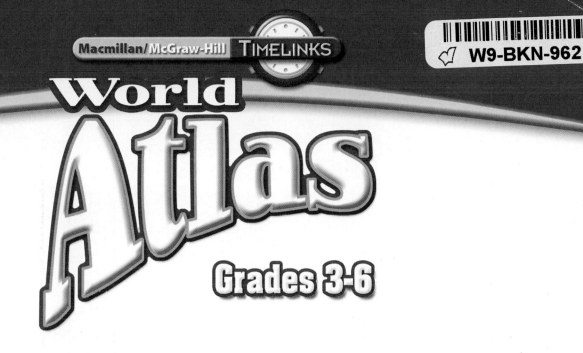

Macmillan/McGraw-Hill **TIMELINKS**

World Atlas

Grades 3-6

Table of Contents

 Macmillan/McGraw-Hill

Dictionary of Geographic Terms

1. **BASIN** A bowl-shaped landform surrounded by higher land

2. **BAY** Part of an ocean or lake that extends deeply into the land

3. **CANAL** A channel built to carry water for irrigation or transportation

4. **CANYON** A deep, narrow valley with steep sides

5. **COAST** The land along an ocean

6. **DAM** A wall built across a river, creating a lake that stores water

7. **DELTA** Land made of soil left behind as a river drains into a larger body of water

8. **DESERT** A dry environment with few plants and animals

9. **FAULT** The border between two of the plates that make up Earth's crust

10. **GLACIER** A huge sheet of ice that moves slowly across the land

11. **GULF** Part of an ocean that extends into the land; larger than a bay

12. **HARBOR** A sheltered place along a coast where boats dock safely

13. **HILL** A rounded, raised landform; not as high as a mountain

14. **ISLAND** A body of land completely surrounded by water

15. **LAKE** A body of water completely surrounded by land

16. **MESA** A hill with a flat top; smaller than a plateau

17 **MOUNTAIN** A high landform with steep sides; higher than a hill

18 **MOUNTAIN PASS** A narrow gap through a mountain range

19 **MOUTH** The place where a river empties into a larger body of water

20 **OCEAN** A large body of salt water; oceans cover much of the Earth's surface

21 **PENINSULA** A body of land nearly surrounded by water

22 **PLAIN** A large area of nearly flat land

23 **PLATEAU** A high, flat area that rises steeply above the surrounding land

24 **PORT** A place where ships load and unload their goods

25 **RESERVOIR** A natural or artificial lake used to store water

26 **RIVER** A stream of water that flows across the land and empties into another body of water

27 **SOURCE** The starting point of a river

28 **VALLEY** An area of low land between hills or mountains

29 **VOLCANO** An opening in Earth's surface through which hot rock and ash are forced out

30 **WATERFALL** A flow of water falling vertically

World: Political

80°N

160°W 120°W 80°W

60°N

ALASKA
(U.S.)

CANADA

NORTH
AMERICA

UNITED STATES

BERMUDA
(U.K.)

ATLANTIC
OCEAN

40°N

MIDWAY ISLANDS
(UnitedaStates)

Tropic of Cancer

20°N

HAWAII
(United States)

MEXICO

See inset below

Caribbean Sea

PACIFIC OCEAN

VENEZUELA

GUYANA
SURINAME
FRENCH
GUIANA
(France)

GALAPAGOS ISLANDS
(Ecuador)

COLOMBIA

0° Equator

ECUADOR

SOUTH
AMERICA

PERU

BRAZIL

AMERICAN
SAMOA
(United
States)

COOK
ISLANDS
(New
Zealand)

BOLIVIA

SAMOA

FRENCH POLYNESIA
(France)

PARAGUAY

TONGA

20°S

PITCAIRN
ISLAND
(United Kingdom)

Tropic of Capricorn

CHILE

URUGUAY

ARGENTINA

40°S

FALKLAND
ISLANDS
(United Kingdom)

60°S

Antarctic Circle

120°W

80°W

160°W

60°W

Central America and West Indies

90°W   80°W   70°W

Gulf of Mexico

FLORIDA
(United States)

0   200   400 miles

0   200   400 kilometers

Tropic of Cancer

BAHAMAS

ATLANTIC
OCEAN

20°N

TURKS &
CAICOS
ISLANDS
(United Kingdom)

VIRGIN IS.
(United Kingdom)

20°N

CUBA

PUERTO RICO
(United States)

ST. KITTS & NEVIS

MEXICO

CAYMAN IS.
(United Kingdom)

HAITI

DOMINICAN
REPUBLIC

ANTIGUA &
BARBUDA

BELIZE

JAMAICA

VIRGIN IS. (United States)

GUADELOUPE
(France)

GUATEMALA

MONTSERRAT (United Kingdom)

HONDURAS

Caribbean Sea

DOMINICA

MARTINIQUE
(France)

EL
SALVADOR

NICARAGUA

NETHERLANDS ANTILLES
(Netherlands)

ST. LUCIA
ST. VINCENT &
THE GRENADINES

BARBADOS

N

W   E

S

ARUBA (Netherlands)

GRENADA

TRINIDAD
& TOBAGO

10°N

60°W

COSTA
RICA

PANAMA

COLOMBIA

VENEZUELA

GUYANA

PACIFIC
OCEAN

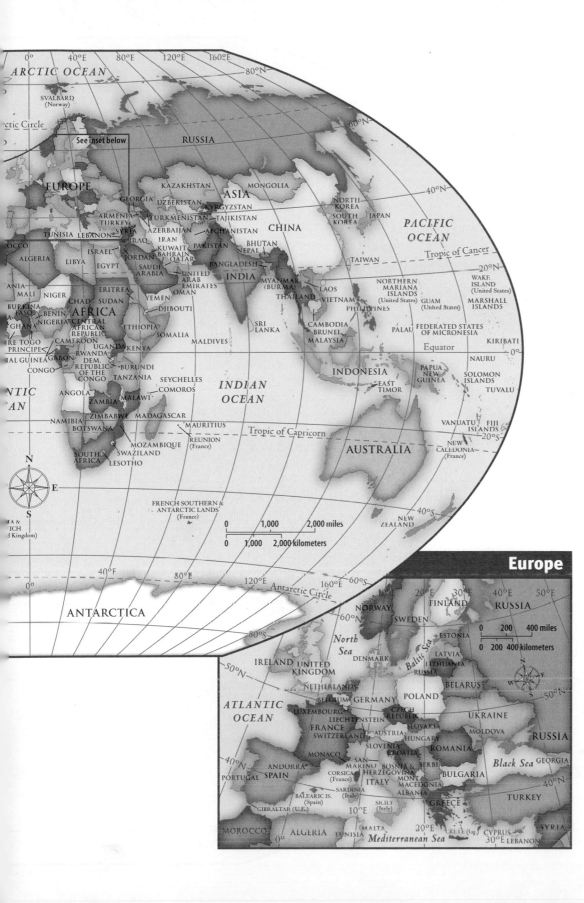

ARCTIC OCEAN

0°   40°E   80°E   120°E   160°E   80°N

SVALBARD
(Norway)

rctic Circle   60°N

See inset below   RUSSIA

EUROPE   KAZAKHSTAN   ASIA   MONGOLIA   40°N

GEORGIA   UZBEKISTAN   KYRGYZSTAN   NORTH
KOREA   JAPAN   PACIFIC
OCEAN

ARMENIA   TURKMENISTAN   TAJIKISTAN   SOUTH
KOREA

TUNISIA   LEBANON   SYRIA   AZERBAIJAN   AFGHANISTAN   CHINA

TURKEY   IRAN   Tropic of Cancer

OCCO   IRAQ   KUWAIT   PAKISTAN   BHUTAN   TAIWAN   20°N

ALGERIA   LIBYA   ISRAEL   JORDAN   BAHRAIN   QATAR   NEPAL
BANGLADESH

EGYPT   SAUDI
ARABIA   UNITED
ARAB
EMIRATES   INDIA   MYANMAR
(BURMA)   LAOS   NORTHERN
MARIANA
ISLANDS
(United States)   WAKE
ISLAND
(United States)

ANIA   OMAN   THAILAND   VIETNAM   GUAM
(United States)   MARSHALL
ISLANDS

MALI   NIGER   CHAD   SUDAN   YEMEN   PHILIPPINES

BURKINA
FASO   BENIN   AFRICA   DJIBOUTI   SRI
LANKA   CAMBODIA   PALAU   FEDERATED STATES
OF MICRONESIA

GHANA   NIGERIA   CENTRAL
AFRICAN
REPUBLIC   ETHIOPIA   SOMALIA   BRUNEI
MALAYSIA   KIRIBATI

RE TOGO   CAMEROON   UGANDA   KENYA   MALDIVES   Equator   0°

PRINCIPE   GABON   RWANDA   NAURU

AL GUINEA   CONGO   DEM.
REPUBLIC
OF THE
CONGO   BURUNDI
TANZANIA   SEYCHELLES   INDONESIA   PAPUA
NEW
GUINEA   SOLOMON
ISLANDS

NTIC   COMOROS   INDIAN
OCEAN   EAST
TIMOR   TUVALU

AN   ANGOLA   ZAMBIA   MALAWI

NAMIBIA   ZIMBABWE   MADAGASCAR   VANUATU   FIJI
ISLANDS   20°S

BOTSWANA   MAURITIUS   Tropic of Capricorn   NEW
CALEDONIA
(France)

SOUTH
AFRICA   SWAZILAND   MOZAMBIQUE   REUNION
(France)   AUSTRALIA

N   LESOTHO

W   E

S   FRENCH SOUTHERN &
ANTARCTIC LANDS
(France)   40°S

0   1,000   2,000 miles   NEW
ZEALAND

0   1,000   2,000 kilometers

IA &
ICH
d Kingdom)   40°E   80°E   120°E   160°E   60°S

0°   Antarctic Circle

ANTARCTICA   80°S

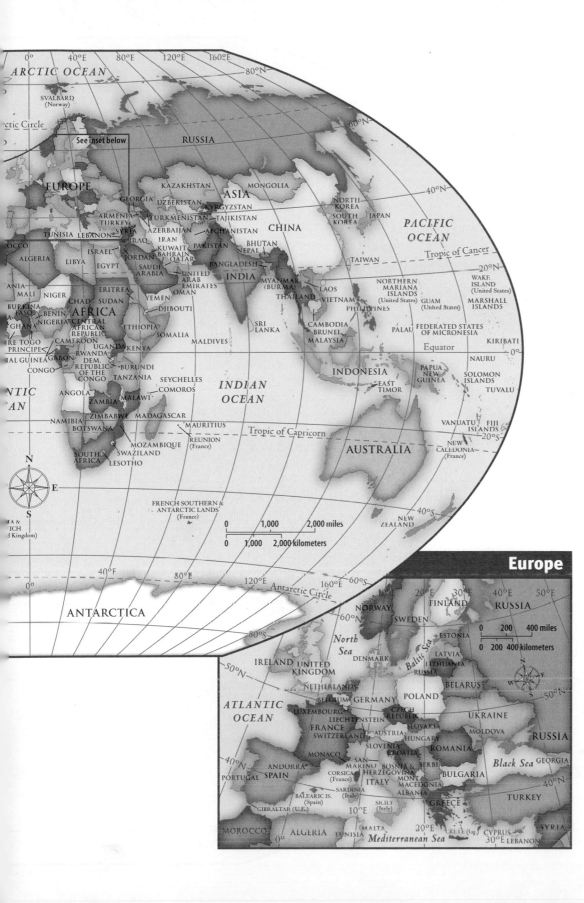

Europe

20°E   30°E   FINLAND   40°E   50°E

NORWAY   RUSSIA

60°N   SWEDEN   ESTONIA   0   200   400 miles

North
Sea   LATVIA   0   200   400 kilometers

IRELAND   UNITED
KINGDOM   DENMARK   LITHUANIA
RUSSIA   BELARUS

NETHERLANDS   50°N

ATLANTIC
OCEAN   BELGIUM   GERMANY   POLAND

LUXEMBOURG   CZECH
REPUBLIC   UKRAINE

LIECHTENSTEIN   SLOVAKIA   MOLDOVA

FRANCE   AUSTRIA   HUNGARY   RUSSIA

SWITZERLAND   SLOVENIA   ROMANIA

MONACO   CROATIA

40°N   SAN
MARINO   BOSNIA &
HERZEGOVINA   SERBIA   Black Sea   GEORGIA

ANDORRA   CORSICA
(France)   ITALY   MONT.   BULGARIA   40°N

PORTUGAL   SPAIN   MACEDONIA

SARDINIA
(Italy)   ALBANIA   TURKEY

BALEARIC IS.
(Spain)   SICILY
(Italy)   GREECE

GIBRALTAR (U.K.)   10°E   MALTA   CYPRUS   SYRIA

MOROCCO   ALGERIA   TUNISIA   20°E   CRETE (Gr.)   30°E   LEBANON

0°   Mediterranean Sea

World: Physical

ARCTIC OCEAN

80°N

160°W   120°W   80°W   40°W

GREENLAND

Mackenzie River

60°N ALASKA RANGE
Mt. McKinley
20,320 ft.
(6,194 m)

Arctic C

ROCKY MOUNTAINS

CANADIAN SHIELD

NORTH AMERICA

40°N

Mississippi River

APPALACHIAN MTS.

PACIFIC OCEAN

ATLANTIC OCEAN

Tropic of Cancer

20°N

Rio Grande

Gulf of Mexico

Caribbean Sea

Equator   0°

Amazon River

SOUTH AMERICA

ANDES

20°S Tropic of Capricorn

Mt. Aconcagua
22,834 ft.
(6,960 m)

MOUNTAINS

ATLANTIC OCEAN

40°S

PACIFIC OCEAN

Cape Horn

60°S Antarctic Circle

80°W   Weddell Sea

120°W Vinson Massif
16,067 ft.
(4,897 m)

160°W   40°W

ARCTIC OCEAN

40°E 80°E 120°E 160°E 80°N

Lena River

Yenisey River

URAL MTS.

Ob River

60°N

Sea of Okhotsk

Volga River

EUROPE

Caspian Sea

ASIA

GOBI

40°N

ALPS

Mont Blanc
15,711 ft.
(4,807 m)

Black Sea ▲ Mt. Elbrus
18,510 ft.
(5,642 m)

HINDU KUSH

Mediterranean Sea

SYRIAN DESERT

HIMALAYA

Yangtze River

Tropic of Cancer

S A H A R A

Ganges River

Mt. Everest
29,035 ft.
(8,850 m)

20°N

Red Sea

DECCAN PLATEAU

Nile

Arabian Sea

Bay of Bengal

South China Sea

Philippine Sea

PACIFIC OCEAN

AFRICA

Congo River

Mt. Kilimanjaro
19,340 ft.
(5,895 m)

Equator 0°

INDIAN OCEAN

Coral Sea

NAMIB DESERT

KALAHARI DESERT

Tropic of Capricorn

GREAT SANDY DESERT

20°S

AUSTRALIA

Cape of Good Hope

Darling River

Mt. Kosciuszko
7,310 ft.
(2,228 m)

N
W   E
S

40°S

0   1,000   2,000 miles
0   1,000   2,000 kilometers

40°E   80°E   120°E   160°E   60°S

Antarctic Circle

ANTARCTICA

North America: Political

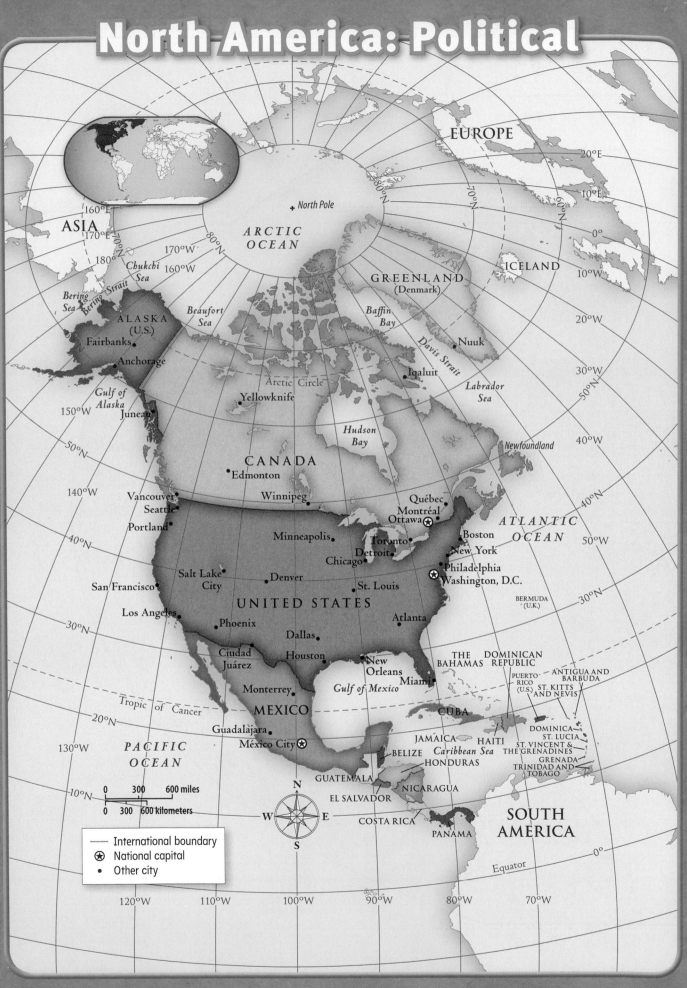

EUROPE

ASIA

ARCTIC OCEAN

+ North Pole

160°E
170°E
180°
170°W
160°W
150°W

Chukchi Sea
Bering Strait
Bering Sea
Beaufort Sea

GREENLAND
(Denmark)

ICELAND

20°E
10°E
0°
10°W
20°W
30°W
40°W

ALASKA (U.S.)
Fairbanks
Anchorage
Gulf of Alaska
Juneau

Baffin Bay
Davis Strait
Nuuk
Iqaluit
Labrador Sea

Arctic Circle
Yellowknife
Hudson Bay

Newfoundland

CANADA
Edmonton
Vancouver
Seattle
Portland
Winnipeg
Québec
Montréal
Ottawa
Boston
New York

ATLANTIC OCEAN

50°W
50°N
40°N

Minneapolis
Toronto
Detroit
Chicago

San Francisco
Los Angeles
Salt Lake City
Denver
St. Louis
Philadelphia
Washington, D.C.

UNITED STATES

BERMUDA (U.K.)

30°N

Phoenix
Dallas
Atlanta

Ciudad Juárez
Houston
New Orleans
Miami

THE BAHAMAS
DOMINICAN REPUBLIC

PUERTO RICO (U.S.)
ANTIGUA AND BARBUDA
ST. KITTS AND NEVIS

Monterrey
Gulf of Mexico

Tropic of Cancer

MEXICO

CUBA

DOMINICA
ST. LUCIA

Guadalajara
México City

JAMAICA
HAITI
Caribbean Sea
BELIZE
HONDURAS

ST. VINCENT & THE GRENADINES
GRENADA
TRINIDAD AND TOBAGO

PACIFIC OCEAN

130°W
120°W
110°W
100°W
90°W
80°W
70°W

0   300   600 miles
0   300   600 kilometers

GUATEMALA
EL SALVADOR
NICARAGUA
COSTA RICA
PANAMA

SOUTH AMERICA

N
W   E
S

Equator

International boundary
⊛ National capital
• Other city

North America: Physical

EUROPE

ASIA

ARCTIC OCEAN

North Pole

Lincoln Sea

Greenland Sea

160°E
170°E
170°W
180°
160°W
150°W
140°W

Chukchi Sea

Point Barrow

Bering Strait
Bering Sea

Beaufort Sea

BROOKS RANGE

Mt. McKinley 20,320 ft. (6,194 m)
Yukon R.
ALASKA RANGE
YUKON PLATEAU

Mackenzie R.

Greenland

Baffin Bay

Davis Strait

Cape Farewell

Arctic Circle

Gulf of Alaska
Mt. Logan 19,551 ft. (5,959 m)

Labrador Sea

Peace R.

Hudson Bay

Churchill R.

Saskatchewan R.
Lake Winnipeg

COAST MOUNTAINS

Vancouver Island

CANADIAN SHIELD

Newfoundland

Gulf of St. Lawrence

ROCKY MOUNTAINS

Snake R.

GREAT BASIN

Missouri River

Great Lakes

Gulf of Maine

Cape Cod

Long Island

ATLANTIC OCEAN

COAST RANGES

Mt. Whitney 14,494 ft. (4,418 m)
Death Valley -282 ft. (-86 m)

Colorado R.

GREAT PLAINS

OZARK PLATEAU

Mississippi R.
Ohio R.

APPALACHIAN MOUNTAINS

Chesapeake Bay

Cape Hatteras

Bermuda (U.K.)

SONORAN DESERT

Gulf of California
BAJA CALIFORNIA

SIERRA MADRE OCCIDENTAL

SIERRA MADRE ORIENTAL

Rio Grande

Red River

COASTAL PLAIN

PACIFIC OCEAN

Tropic of Cancer

Gulf of Mexico

WEST INDIES

Puerto Rico (U.S.)

Orizaba 18,855 ft. (5,747 m)
YUCATÁN PENINSULA

Caribbean Sea

CENTRAL AMERICA

Lake Nicaragua

SOUTH AMERICA

Isthmus of Panama

Equator

80°N
70°N
60°N
50°N
40°N
30°N
20°N
10°N

20°E
10°E
0°
10°W
20°W
30°W
40°W
50°W

120°W
110°W
100°W
90°W
80°W
70°W
130°W

N
W   E
S

0   300   600 miles
0   300   600 kilometers

— International boundary
▲ Mountain peak

South America: Political

CENTRAL AMERICA

Caribbean Sea

Lake Maracaibo

Barranquilla

Maracaibo
Valencia • Caracas

VENEZUELA

GUYANA

SURINAME

Georgetown
Paramaribo

Cayenne

FRENCH GUIANA
(France)

ATLANTIC OCEAN

Gulf of Panama

Medellín

Bogotá

Cali

COLOMBIA

Equator

Quito

ECUADOR

Guayaquil

Galapagos Islands (Ecuador)

Iquitos

Manaus

Belém

Equator

Trujillo

PERU

Callao

Lima

Cuzco

Lake Titicaca

Arequipa

La Paz

BOLIVIA

Sucre

BRAZIL

Recife

Brasília

Salvador (Bahía)

Belo Horizonte

PARAGUAY

São Paulo

Rio de Janeiro

Antofagasta

Asunción

Tropic of Capricorn

Tucumán

CHILE

Córdoba

Rosario

Valparaíso
Santiago

Concepción

ARGENTINA

Buenos Aires

URUGUAY

Montevideo

Río de la Plata

Pôrto Alegre

Tropic of Capricorn

PACIFIC OCEAN

ATLANTIC OCEAN

0   250   500 miles
0   250   500 kilometers

Punta Arenas

Strait of Magellan

Falkland Islands
(Islas Malvinas)
(U.K.)

South Georgia
(U.K.)

— International boundary
⊛ National capital
• Other city

South America: Physical

90°W · 75°W · 60°W

Caribbean Sea

15°N

ISTHMUS OF PANAMA

Lake Maracaibo

Gulf of Panama

Orinoco R.

GUIANA HIGHLANDS

ATLANTIC OCEAN

Negro R.

Equator · 0°

Galapagos Islands (Ecuador)

Amazon R.

AMAZON BASIN

Madeira R.

Tapajós R.

Xingú R.

Tocantins R.

São Francisco R.

A N D E S   M O U N T A I N S

Lake Titicaca

Paraguay R.

BRAZILIAN HIGHLANDS

Paraná R.

15°S

N
W · E
S

ATACAMA DESERT

Mt. Ojos del Salado
22,572 ft.
(6,880 m)

ANDES MOUNTAINS

Paraná

Tropic of Capricorn

Mt. Aconcagua
22,834 ft. (6,960 m)

30°S

PACIFIC OCEAN

PAMPAS

Rio de la Plata

ATLANTIC OCEAN

P A T A G O N I A

0 250 500 miles
0 250 500 kilometers

45°S

Falkland Islands
(Islas Malvinas)
(U.K.)

Strait of Magellan
TIERRA DEL FUEGO

Cape Horn

South Georgia
(U.K.)

International boundary
▲ Mountain peak

105°W · 90°W · 75°W · 60°W · 45°W · 30°W

Africa: Political

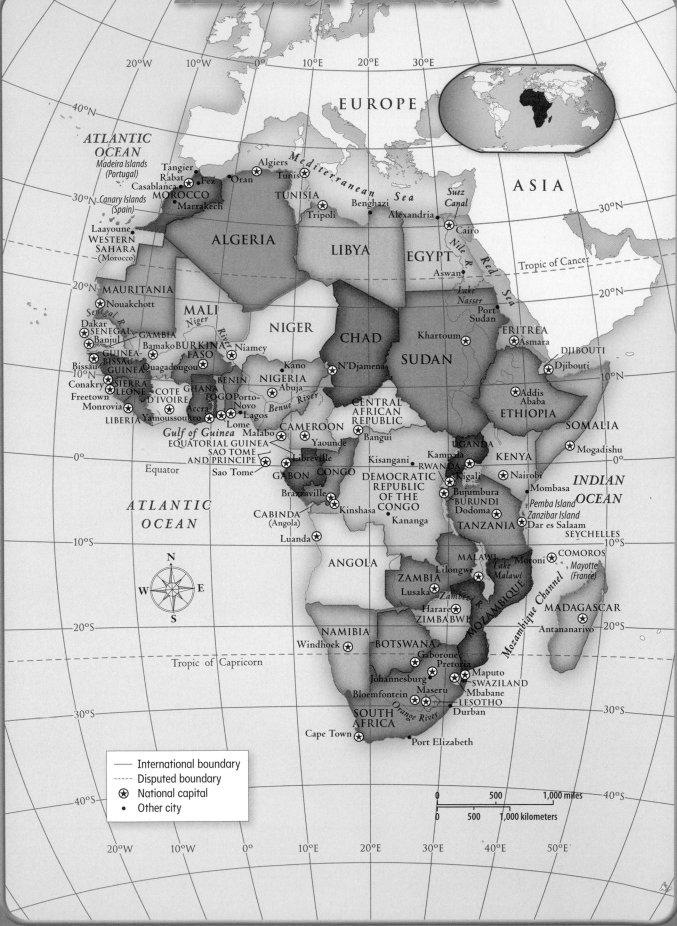

Africa: Physical

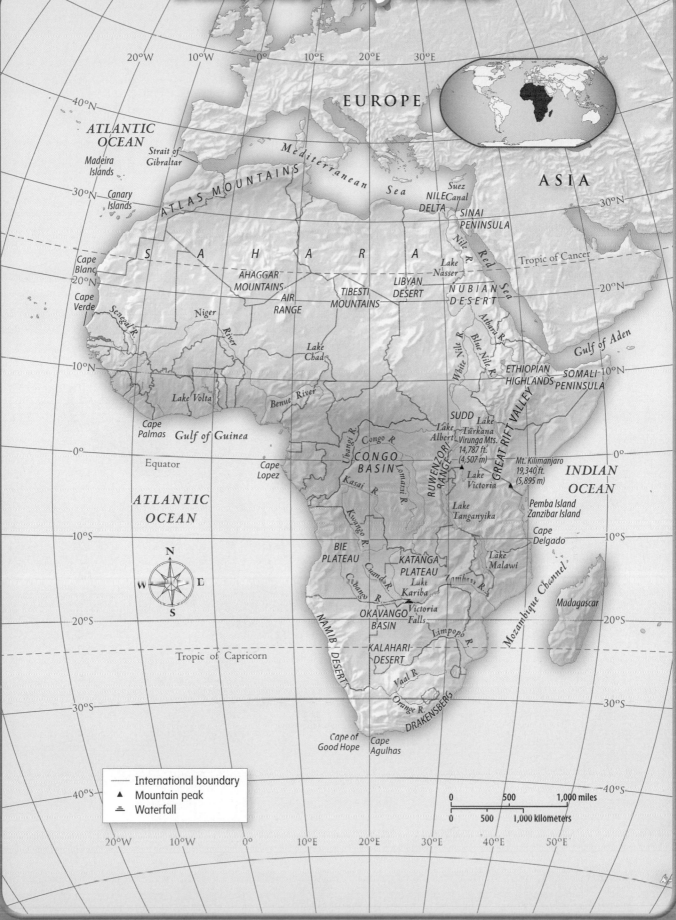

Europe: Political

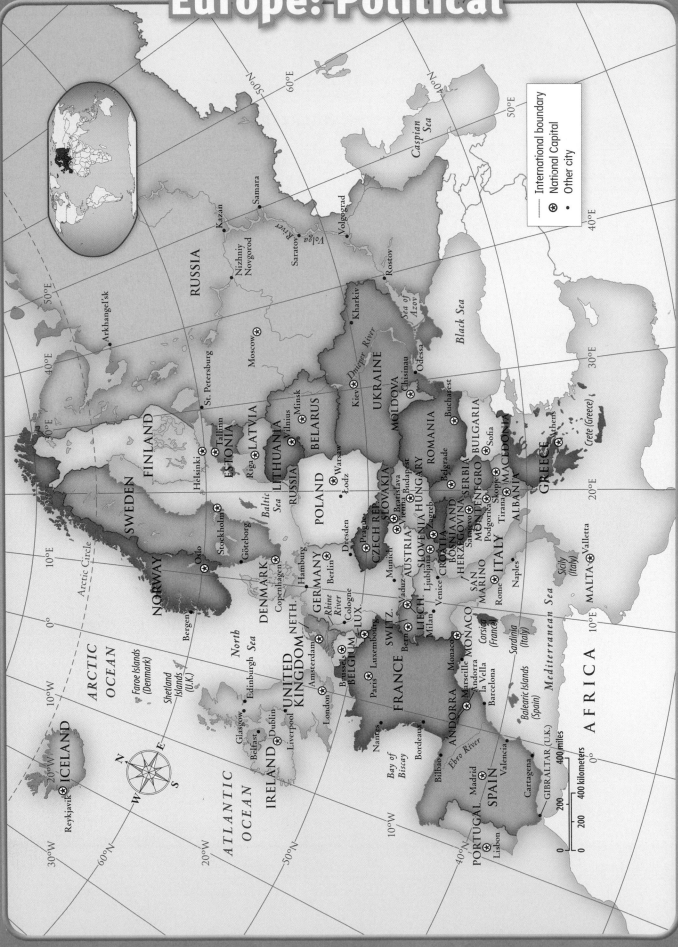

International boundary
⊛ National Capital
• Other city

Map labels:

ARCTIC OCEAN
ATLANTIC OCEAN
ICELAND — Reykjavík
Faroe Islands (Denmark)
Shetland Islands (U.K.)
IRELAND — Dublin, Belfast, Glasgow, Edinburgh, Liverpool, London
UNITED KINGDOM
NORWAY — Oslo, Bergen
SWEDEN — Stockholm, Göteborg
FINLAND — Helsinki
North Sea
Bay of Biscay
RUSSIA — Arkhangel'sk, Moscow, St. Petersburg, Nizhniy Novgorod, Kazan, Samara, Saratov, Volgograd, Rostov
Volga River
Caspian Sea
ESTONIA — Tallinn
LATVIA — Riga
LITHUANIA — Vilnius
BELARUS — Minsk
POLAND — Warsaw, Łódź
Baltic Sea
DENMARK — Copenhagen
GERMANY — Berlin, Hamburg, Dresden, Munich, Cologne
NETH. — Amsterdam
BELGIUM — Brussels
LUX. — Luxembourg
Rhine River
FRANCE — Paris, Nantes, Bordeaux, Marseille
SWITZ. — Bern
LIECH. — Vaduz
AUSTRIA — Vienna
CZECH REP. — Prague
SLOVAKIA — Bratislava
HUNGARY — Budapest
SLOVENIA — Ljubljana
CROATIA — Zagreb
BOSNIA AND HERZEGOVINA — Sarajevo
SERBIA — Belgrade
MONTENEGRO — Podgorica
ALBANIA — Tirana
MACEDONIA — Skopje
BULGARIA — Sofia
ROMANIA — Bucharest
MOLDOVA — Chisinau
UKRAINE — Kiev, Kharkiv, Odessa
Dnieper River
Sea of Azov
Black Sea
GREECE — Athens
Crete (Greece)
ITALY — Rome, Milan, Venice, Naples
SAN MARINO
MONACO — Monaco
Corsica (France)
Sardinia (Italy)
Sicily (Italy)
MALTA — Valletta
Mediterranean Sea
ANDORRA — Andorra la Vella
SPAIN — Madrid, Barcelona, Valencia, Bilbao, Cartagena
Balearic Islands (Spain)
Ebro River
PORTUGAL — Lisbon
GIBRALTAR (U.K.)
AFRICA

Arctic Circle

30°W, 20°W, 10°W, 0°, 10°E, 20°E, 30°E, 40°E, 50°E, 60°E
40°N, 50°N, 60°N, 70°N

N E W S

GIBRALTAR (U.K.)
0 200 400 miles
0 200 400 kilometers

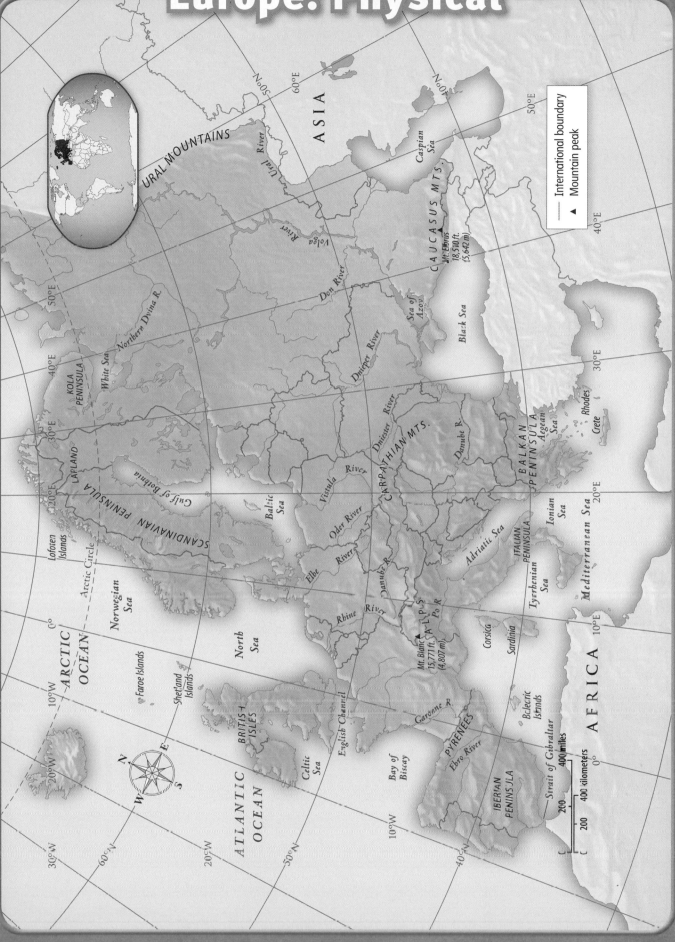

——	International boundary
▲	Mountain peak

ASIA

URAL MOUNTAINS

Ural River

Volga River

Caspian Sea

CAUCASUS MTS.

Mt. Elbrus
18,510 ft.
(5,642 m)

Don River

Sea of Azov

Black Sea

Northern Dvina R.

White Sea

KOLA PENINSULA

Dnieper River

Dniester River

CARPATHIAN MTS.

Danube R.

BALKAN PENINSULA

Aegean Sea

Rhodes

Crete

LAPLAND

Gulf of Bothnia

SCANDINAVIAN PENINSULA

Vistula River

Oder River

Baltic Sea

Elbe River

Danube R.

Adriatic Sea

ITALIAN PENINSULA

Ionian Sea

Mediterranean Sea

Lofoten Islands

Arctic Circle

Norwegian Sea

Rhine River

A L P S

Po R.

Corsica

Sardinia

Tyrrhenian Sea

Mt. Blanc
15,771 ft.
(4,807 m)

ARCTIC OCEAN

0°

10°W

Faroe Islands

Shetland Islands

North Sea

BRITISH ISLES

English Channel

Celtic Sea

Bay of Biscay

ATLANTIC OCEAN

Garonne R.

PYRENEES

Ebro River

Balearic Islands

Strait of Gibraltar

IBERIAN PENINSULA

AFRICA

N
W   E
S

30°W

20°W

10°W

0°

10°E

20°E

30°E

40°E

50°E

60°E

70°N

60°N

50°N

40°N

400 miles
400 kilometers
200
200

Asia: Political

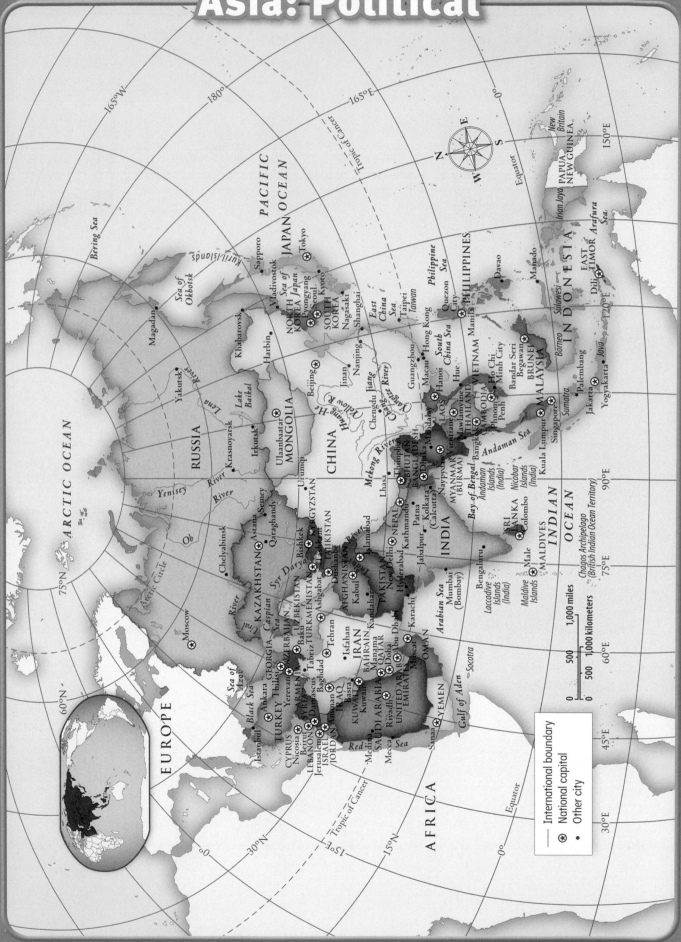

Asia: Physical

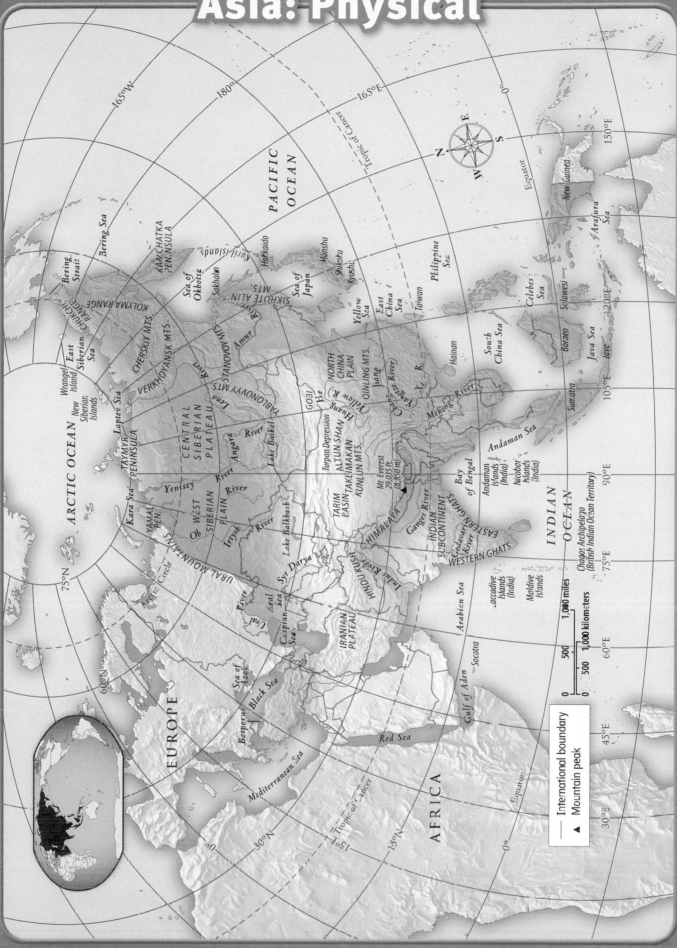

PACIFIC OCEAN

ARCTIC OCEAN

INDIAN OCEAN

EUROPE

AFRICA

Bering Strait
Bering Sea
CHUKCHI RANGE
KOLYMA RANGE
KAMCHATKA PENINSULA
Sea of Okhotsk
Kuril Islands
Sakhalin
SIKHOTE ALIN MTS.
Sea of Japan
Hokkaido
Honshu
Shikoku
Kyushu
Amur River
STANOVOY MTS.
YABLONOVYY MTS.
CHERSKIY MTS.
VERKHOYANSK MTS.
Wrangel Island
New Siberian Islands
East Siberian Sea
Laptev Sea
TAYMYR PENINSULA
CENTRAL SIBERIAN PLATEAU
Lena River
Angara River
Lake Baikal
Yenisey
Ob
WEST SIBERIAN PLAIN
Irtysh River
Kara Sea
YAMAL PEN.
Ural River
Aral Sea
Caspian Sea
URAL MOUNTAINS
Syr Darya
Lake Balkhash
Arctic Circle
GOBI
Huang He (Yellow R.)
NORTH CHINA PLAIN
QINLING MTS.
Yellow Sea
East China Sea
Taiwan
Hainan
South China Sea
Chang Jiang (Yangtze River)
Mekong River
Philippine Sea
Turpan Depression
ALTUN SHAN
TARIM BASIN
TAKLIMAKAN
KUNLUN MTS.
Mt Everest 29,035 ft. (8,850 m)
HIMALAYA
HINDU KUSH
Indus River
Ganges River
INDIAN SUBCONTINENT
Godavari River
EASTERN GHATS
WESTERN GHATS
Bay of Bengal
Andaman Sea
Andaman Islands (India)
Nicobar Islands (India)
Sumatra
Borneo
Java Sea
Java
Celebes Sea
Sulawesi
Arafura Sea
New Guinea
IRANIAN PLATEAU
Arabian Sea
Laccadive Islands (India)
Maldive Islands
Chagos Archipelago (British Indian Ocean Territory)
Socotra
Gulf of Aden
Red Sea
Mediterranean Sea
Black Sea
Sea of Azov
Bosporus
Tropic of Cancer
Equator
Tropic of Capricorn

Compass rose: N E S W

165°W
180°
165°E
150°E
135°E
120°E
105°E
90°E
75°E
60°E
45°E
30°E
0°
75°N
60°N
30°N
15°N

Legend
— International boundary
▲ Mountain peak

1,000 miles
500
0
1,000 kilometers
500
0

Middle East: Political/Physical

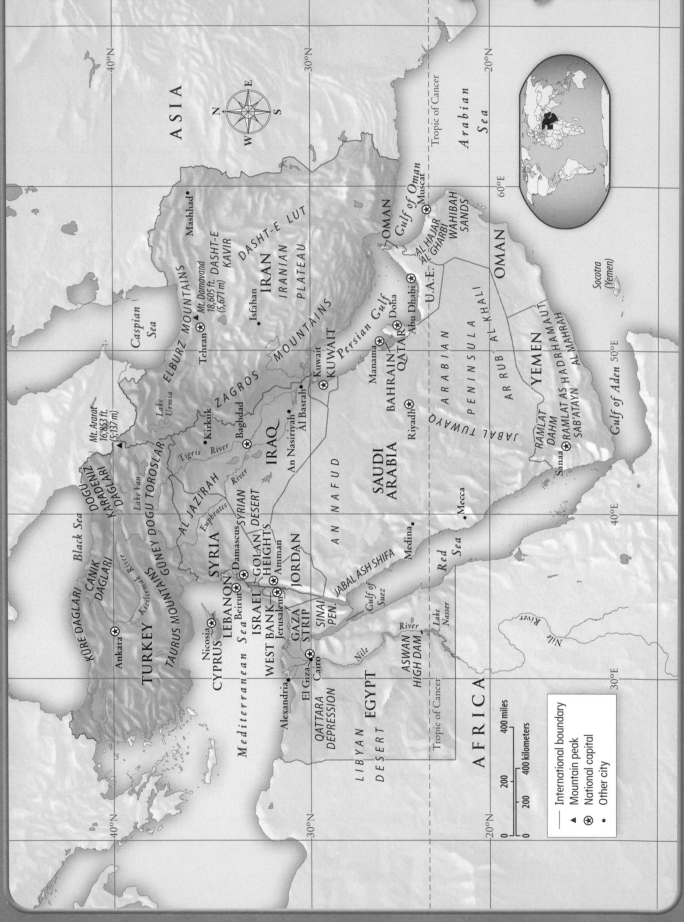

18

Antarctica: Political/Physical

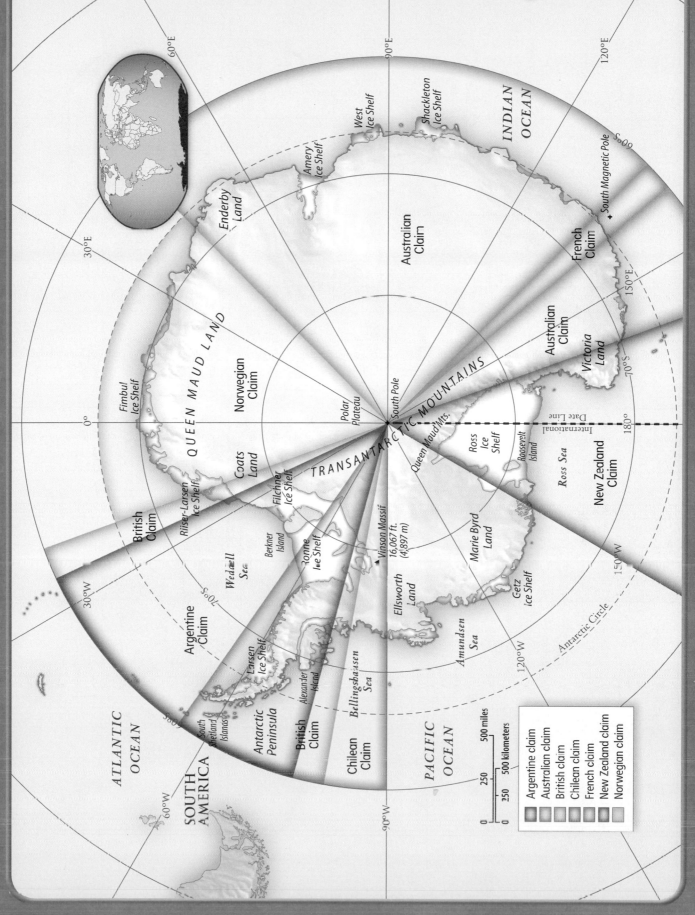

60°E

90°E

120°E

INDIAN OCEAN

Shackleton Ice Shelf

West Ice Shelf

Amery Ice Shelf

Enderby Land

Australian Claim

South Magnetic Pole

French Claim

60°S

150°E

Australian Claim

Victoria Land

70°S

30°E

QUEEN MAUD LAND

Norwegian Claim

Polar Plateau

South Pole

TRANSANTARCTIC MOUNTAINS

Queen Maud Mts.

Ross Ice Shelf

Roosevelt Island

International Date Line

180°

Ross Sea

New Zealand Claim

0°

Fimbul Ice Shelf

Coats Land

Filchner Ice Shelf

Riiser-Larsen Ice Shelf

British Claim

Berkner Island

Weddell Sea

Ronne Ice Shelf

Vinson Massif 16,067 ft. (4,897 m)

Ellsworth Land

Marie Byrd Land

Getz Ice Shelf

150°W

30°W

70°S

Argentine Claim

Larsen Ice Shelf

Alexander Island

Bellingshausen Sea

Amundsen Sea

120°W

Antarctic Circle

ATLANTIC OCEAN

60°W

SOUTH AMERICA

60°S

South Shetland Islands

Antarctic Peninsula

British Claim

Chilean Claim

PACIFIC OCEAN

90°W

250 500 miles
250 500 kilometers
0

Argentine claim
Australian claim
British claim
Chilean claim
French claim
New Zealand claim
Norwegian claim

Australia and Oceania: Political

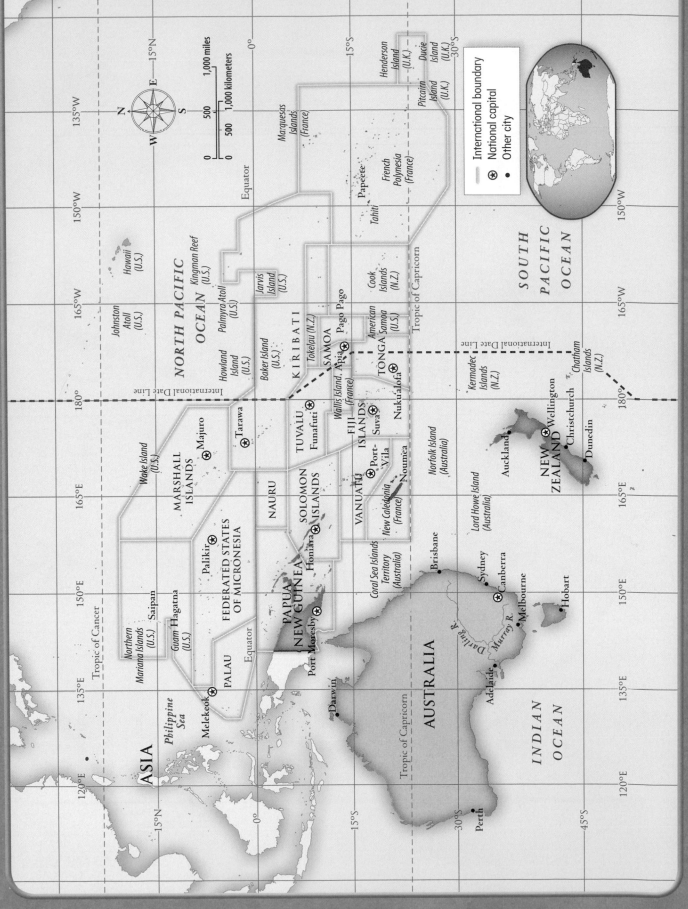

International boundary
National capital ⊛
Other city •

1,000 miles
1,000 kilometers
500
500
0
0

N
W E
S

15°N
0°
15°S
30°S

135°W
150°W
165°W
180°
165°E
150°E
135°E
120°E

NORTH PACIFIC OCEAN

SOUTH PACIFIC OCEAN

Henderson Island (U.K.)
Ducie Island (U.K.)
Pitcairn Island (U.K.)
Marquesas Islands (France)
Papeete
Tahiti
French Polynesia (France)

Hawaii (U.S.)
Kingman Reef (U.S.)
Johnston Atoll (U.S.)
Jarvis Island (U.S.)
Palmyra Atoll (U.S.)
Cook Islands (N.Z.)

Tropic of Capricorn

Howland Island (U.S.)
Baker Island (U.S.)
KIRIBATI
Pago Pago
American Samoa (U.S.)

International Date Line

Tokelau (N.Z.)
SAMOA
Apia ⊛
TONGA
Nuku'alofa ⊛
Kermadec Islands (N.Z.)
Chatham Islands (N.Z.)

Wake Island (U.S.)
MARSHALL ISLANDS
Majuro ⊛
Tarawa ⊛
TUVALU
Funafuti ⊛
FIJI ISLANDS
Suva ⊛
Wallis Island (France)
Christchurch
Wellington ⊛
Dunedin
NEW ZEALAND
Auckland

Saipan
Northern Mariana Islands (U.S.)
Guam Hagåtña (U.S.)
FEDERATED STATES OF MICRONESIA
Palikir ⊛
NAURU
SOLOMON ISLANDS
Honiara ⊛
Port-Vila ⊛
VANUATU
Nouméa
New Caledonia (France)
Norfolk Island (Australia)
Lord Howe Island (Australia)

Tropic of Cancer

ASIA
Philippine Sea
Melekeok ⊛
PALAU
Equator
PAPUA NEW GUINEA
Port Moresby ⊛
Coral Sea Islands Territory (Australia)

Brisbane
Sydney
Canberra ⊛
Melbourne
Hobart

AUSTRALIA
Darling R.
Murray R.
Adelaide
Tropic of Capricorn
Darwin
INDIAN OCEAN
Perth

Equator
15°N
0°
15°S
30°S
45°S

120°E
135°E
150°E
165°E
180°
165°W
150°W

20

Australia and Oceania: Physical

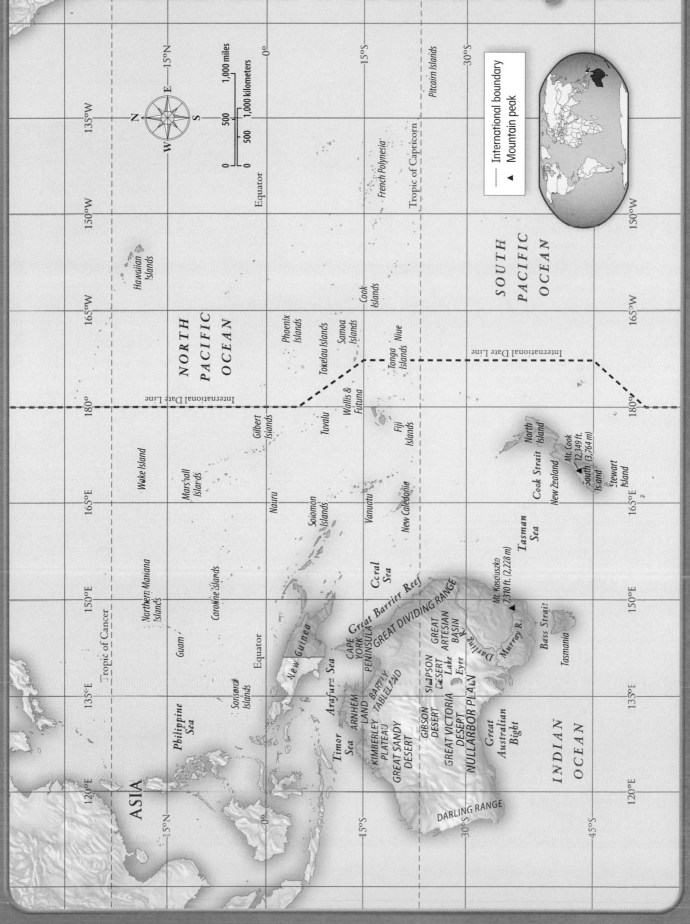

International boundary
▲ Mountain peak

1,000 miles
1,000 kilometers
500
500

N
W E
S

15°N
0°
15°S
30°S

135°W
150°W
165°W
180°
165°E
150°E
135°E
120°E

Equator

NORTH PACIFIC OCEAN

Hawaiian Islands

Phoenix Islands
Tokelau Islands
Samoa Islands
Cook Islands

French Polynesia

Pitcairn Islands

Tropic of Capricorn

SOUTH PACIFIC OCEAN

International Date Line

Tonga Islands
Niue

Wallis & Futuna

Gilbert Islands
Tuvalu

Fiji Islands

Wake Island

Marshall Islands

Nauru

Solomon Islands

Vanuatu

New Caledonia

North Island

Mt. Cook 12,349 ft. (3,764 m)
South Island
New Zealand
Cook Strait
Stewart Island

Tasman Sea

Tropic of Cancer

Northern Mariana Islands

Guam

Caroline Islands

Philippine Sea

Sonsorol Islands

New Guinea

Arafura Sea

Timor Sea

Coral Sea

Great Barrier Reef

CAPE YORK PENINSULA
GREAT DIVIDING RANGE

ARNHEM LAND
BARKLY TABLELAND

KIMBERLEY PLATEAU

GREAT SANDY DESERT

GIBSON DESERT

GREAT VICTORIA DESERT

SIMPSON DESERT

Lake Eyre

GREAT ARTESIAN BASIN

NULLARBOR PLAIN

Great Australian Bight

Mt. Kosciuszko 7,310 ft. (2,228 m) ▲

Darling R.

Murray R.

Bass Strait

Tasmania

INDIAN OCEAN

DARLING RANGE

ASIA

Equator

15°N
0°
15°S
30°S
45°S

120°E
135°E
150°E
165°E
165°W
150°W

21

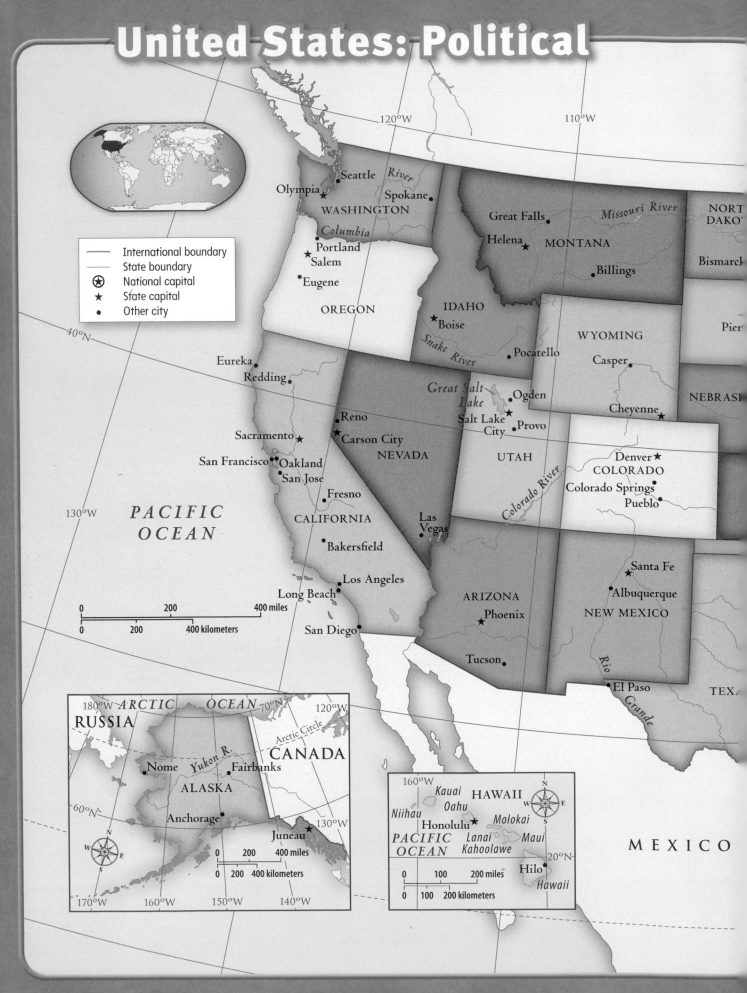

International boundary
State boundary
National capital
State capital
Other city

Seattle
Olympia
WASHINGTON
Spokane
Columbia
Portland
Salem
Eugene
OREGON

River
Great Falls
Helena
MONTANA
Billings
Missouri River
NORTH DAKOTA
Bismarck

IDAHO
Boise
Snake River
Pocatello
WYOMING
Casper
Pier

Eureka
Redding
Reno
Sacramento
Carson City
NEVADA
San Francisco
Oakland
San Jose
Fresno
CALIFORNIA
Bakersfield
Los Angeles
Long Beach
San Diego

Great Salt Lake
Ogden
Salt Lake City
Provo
UTAH
Colorado River

Cheyenne
NEBRASKA

Denver
COLORADO
Colorado Springs
Pueblo

PACIFIC OCEAN

Las Vegas

ARIZONA
Phoenix
Tucson

Santa Fe
Albuquerque
NEW MEXICO

Rio Grande
El Paso
TEXAS

120°W   110°W
40°N
130°W
20°N

0   200   400 miles
0   200   400 kilometers

ARCTIC OCEAN
180°W   70°N
RUSSIA   120°W
Arctic Circle
CANADA
Nome   Yukon R.   Fairbanks
ALASKA
60°N
Anchorage
130°W
Juneau
170°W   160°W   150°W   140°W
0   200   400 miles
0   200   400 kilometers

160°W
Kauai   HAWAII
Oahu
Niihau
Honolulu   Molokai
PACIFIC OCEAN   Lanai   Maui
Kahoolawe
Hilo
Hawaii
0   100   200 miles
0   100   200 kilometers

MEXICO

United States: Physical

Legend:
- International boundary
- State boundary
- ▲ Mountain peak
- ▲ Highest point
- ▼ Lowest point

Puget Sound
Mt. Rainier 14,410 ft. (4,392 m) ▲
Mt. St. Helens 8,363 ft. (2,549 m) ▲
Columbia R.
Mt. Hood 11,239 ft. (3,426 m) ▲
Mt. Shasta 14,162 ft. (4,317 m) ▲
CASCADE RANGE
COLUMBIA PLATEAU
ROCKY
Missouri River
Granite Peak 12,799 ft. (3,901 m) ▲
BLACK HILLS
Snake River
Platte River
Cape Mendocino
Sacramento R.
San Joaquin R.
CENTRAL VALLEY
SIERRA NEVADA
COAST RANGES
San Francisco Bay
Lake Tahoe
GREAT BASIN
Great Salt Lake
GREAT SALT LAKE DESERT
WASATCH RANGE
Kings Peak 13,528 ft. (4,123 m) ▲
Mt. Elbert 14,433 ft. (4,399 m) ▲
Pikes Peak 14,110 ft. (4,301 m) ▲
COLORADO
Mt. Whitney 14,494 ft. (4,418 m) ▲
Death Valley -282 ft. (-86 m) ▼
Lake Mead
PLATEAU
Wheeler Peak 13,161 ft. (4,011 m) ▲
MOUNTAINS
PACIFIC OCEAN
MOJAVE DESERT
Salton Sea
Channel Islands
Colorado River
Humphreys Peak 12,633 ft. (3,851 m) ▲
Gila River
SONORAN DESERT
CONTINENTAL DIVIDE
Guadalupe Peak 8,749 ft. (2,667 m) ▲
Pecos River
Rio Grande
MEXICO

Scale:
0 200 400 miles
0 200 400 kilometers

120°W, 110°W, 130°W, 120°W, 40°N

Alaska inset
180°W
ARCTIC OCEAN
70°N
120°W
RUSSIA
BROOKS RANGE
ALASKA
Arctic Circle
CANADA
Mt. McKinley 20,320 ft. (6,194 m) ▲
Bering Strait
Bering Sea
60°N
ALASKA RANGE
Yukon River
130°W
Gulf of Alaska
0 200 400 miles
0 200 400 kilometers
Aleutian Islands
170°W 160°W 150°W 140°W

Hawaii inset
160°W
Kauai
HAWAII
N
W E
S
Niihau
Oahu
Molokai
PACIFIC OCEAN
Lanai
Kahoolawe
Maui
20°N
Hawaii
0 100 200 miles
0 100 200 kilometers

CANADA

Lake of the Woods

MESABI RANGE

Lake Superior

GREAT LAKES

Mississippi River

Lake Michigan

Lake Huron

Lake Ontario

St. Lawrence River

GREEN MOUNTAINS

Mt. Washington
6,288 ft.
(1,917 m)

ADIRONDACK MOUNTAINS

Hudson River

Cape Cod

Lake Erie

ALLEGHENY PLATEAU

ALLEGHENY MOUNTAINS

Susquehanna River

Long Island

Delaware Bay

CENTRAL PLAINS

River

Wabash River

Ohio

River

A P P A L A C H I A N   M O U N T A I N S

PIEDMONT

Potomac River

Chesapeake Bay

Cape Hatteras

Missouri River

GREAT PLAINS

Arkansas River

INTERIOR PLAINS

OZARK PLATEAU

OUACHITA MOUNTAINS

Red River

Mississippi River

Tennessee River

Mt. Mitchell
6,684 ft.
(2,037 m)

Savannah River

ATLANTIC COASTAL PLAIN

ATLANTIC OCEAN

Brazos River

Colorado River

EDWARDS PLATEAU

Alabama River

Chattahoochee River

GULF COASTAL PLAIN

Galveston Bay

Mobile Bay

Mississippi River Delta

Gulf of Mexico

Lake Okeechobee

BAHAMAS

Florida Keys

Straits of Florida

Tropic of Cancer

CUBA

N
W   E
S

50°N

90°W   80°W   70°W

40°N

70°W

30°N

80°W

90°W

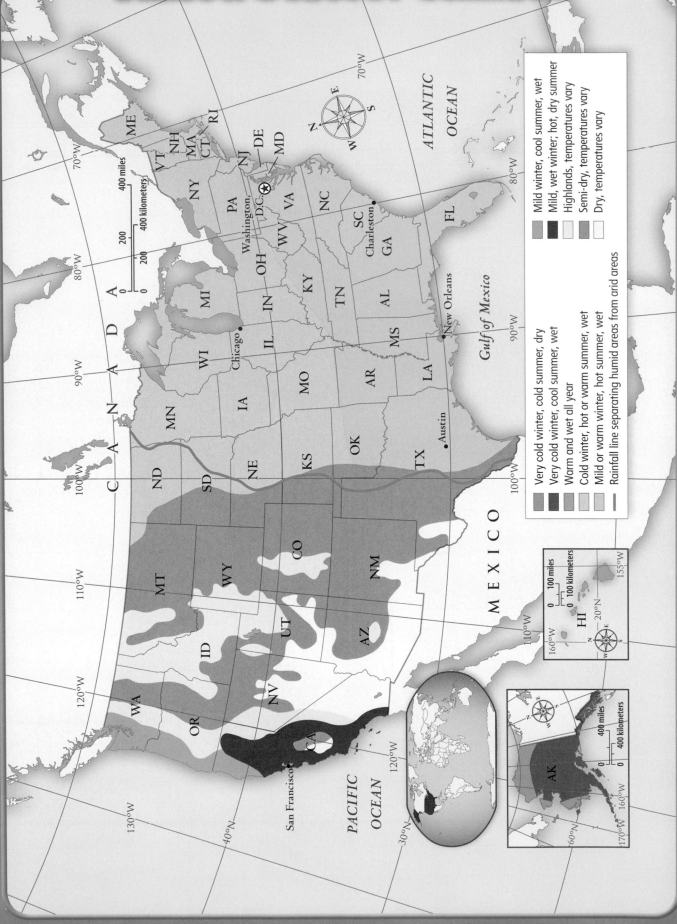

Legend:
- Very cold winter, cold summer, dry
- Very cold winter, cool summer, wet
- Warm and wet all year
- Cold winter, hot or warm summer, wet
- Mild or warm winter, hot summer, wet
- Rainfall line separating humid areas from arid areas

- Mild winter, cool summer, wet
- Mild, wet winter; hot, dry summer
- Highlands, temperatures vary
- Semi-dry, temperatures vary
- Dry, temperatures vary

CANADA

MEXICO

ATLANTIC OCEAN

PACIFIC OCEAN

Gulf of Mexico

ME, NH, VT, MA, CT, RI, NY, PA, NJ, DE, MD, WV, VA, NC, SC, GA, FL, OH, IN, KY, TN, AL, MS, LA, AR, MO, IA, IL, WI, MI, MN, ND, SD, NE, KS, OK, TX, CO, NM, WY, MT, UT, AZ, ID, NV, WA, OR, CA

Washington, D.C., Charleston, New Orleans, Austin, Chicago, San Francisco

HI, AK

400 miles
400 kilometers
200
200
0
0

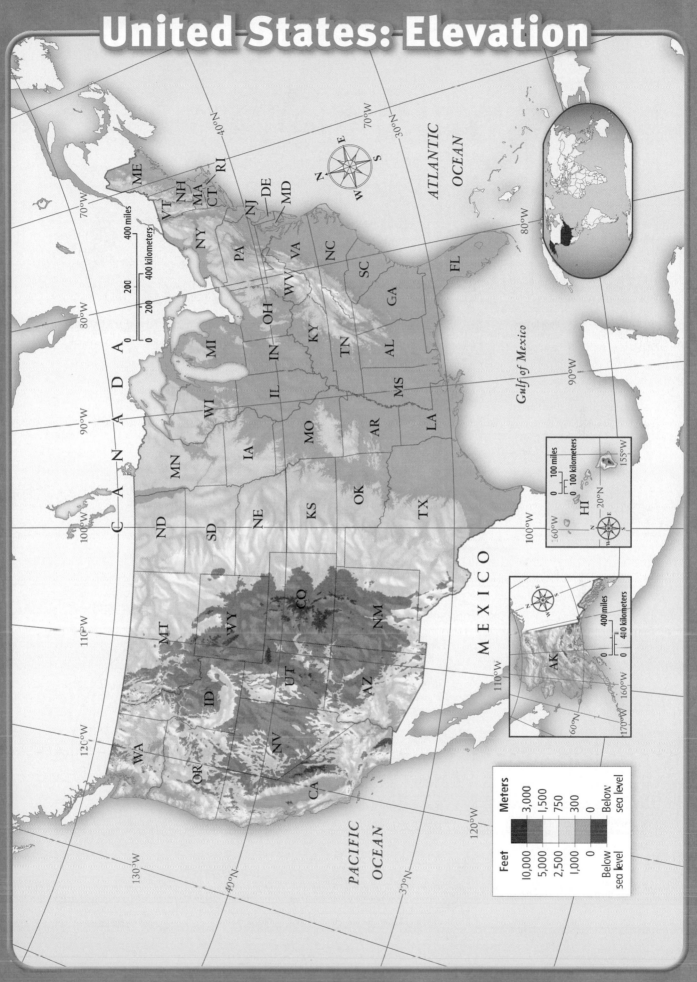

United States Population

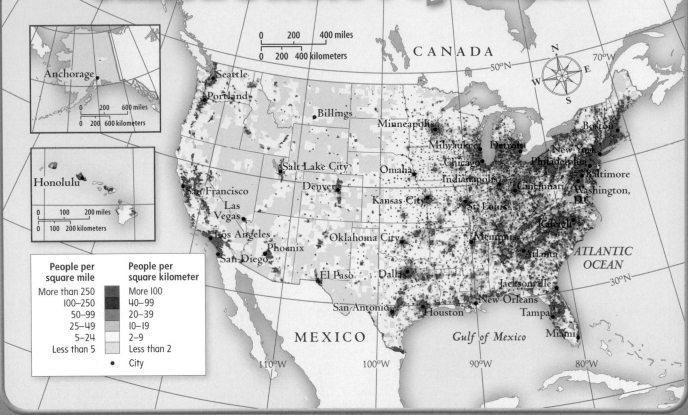

People per square mile
- More than 250
- 100–250
- 50–99
- 25–49
- 5–24
- Less than 5

People per square kilometer
- More 100
- 40–99
- 20–39
- 10–19
- 2–9
- Less than 2

- • City

World Population

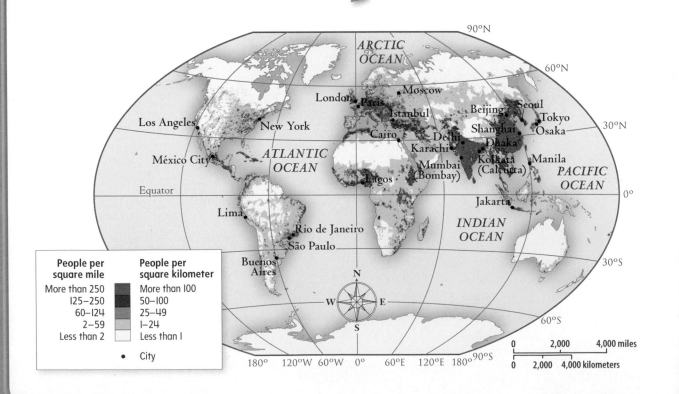

People per square mile
- More than 250
- 125–250
- 60–124
- 2–59
- Less than 2

People per square kilometer
- More than 100
- 50–100
- 25–49
- 1–24
- Less than 1

- • City

Time Zones of North America

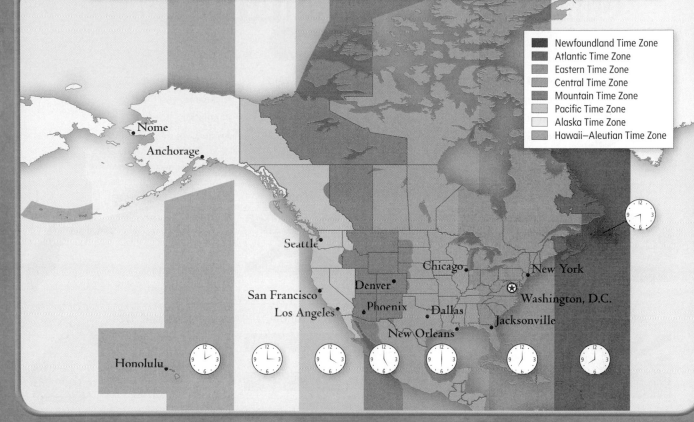

Newfoundland Time Zone
Atlantic Time Zone
Eastern Time Zone
Central Time Zone
Mountain Time Zone
Pacific Time Zone
Alaska Time Zone
Hawaii–Aleutian Time Zone

World Time Zones

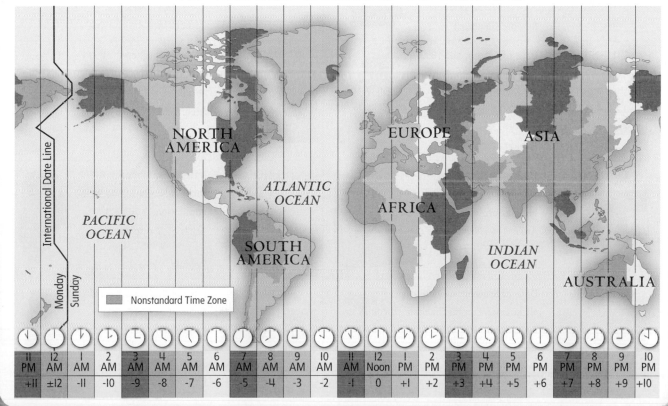

	11 PM	12 AM	1 AM	2 AM	3 AM	4 AM	5 AM	6 AM	7 AM	8 AM	9 AM	10 AM	11 AM	12 Noon	1 PM	2 PM	3 PM	4 PM	5 PM	6 PM	7 PM	8 PM	9 PM	10 PM
	+11	±12	-11	-10	-9	-8	-7	-6	-5	-4	-3	-2	-1	0	+1	+2	+3	+4	+5	+6	+7	+8	+9	+10

The 50 States

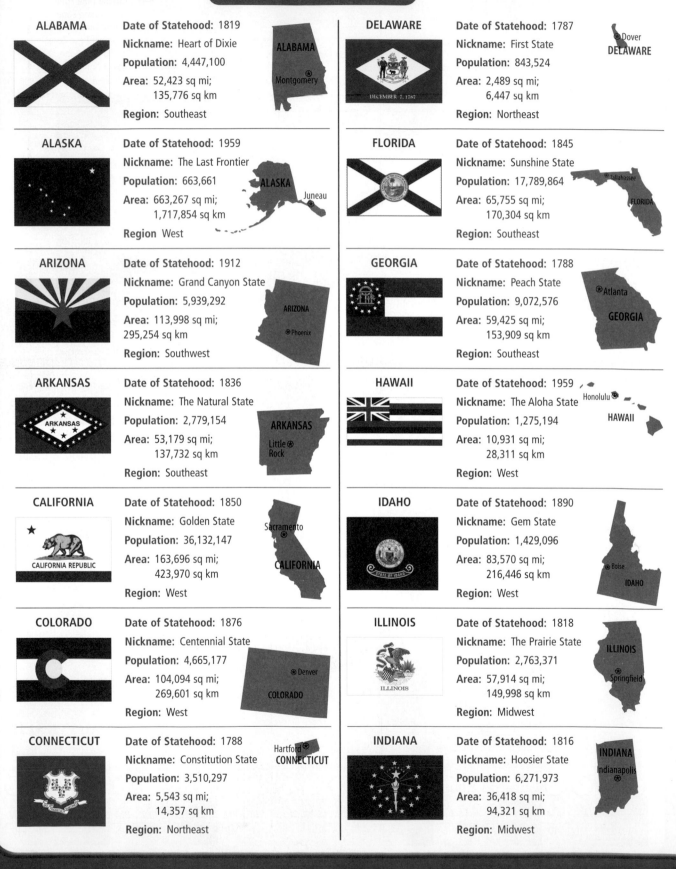

ALABAMA

Date of Statehood: 1819

Nickname: Heart of Dixie

Population: 4,447,100

Area: 52,423 sq mi; 135,776 sq km

Region: Southeast

ALABAMA
Montgomery

ALASKA

Date of Statehood: 1959

Nickname: The Last Frontier

Population: 663,661

Area: 663,267 sq mi; 1,717,854 sq km

Region West

ALASKA
Juneau

ARIZONA

Date of Statehood: 1912

Nickname: Grand Canyon State

Population: 5,939,292

Area: 113,998 sq mi; 295,254 sq km

Region: Southwest

ARIZONA
Phoenix

ARKANSAS

Date of Statehood: 1836

Nickname: The Natural State

Population: 2,779,154

Area: 53,179 sq mi; 137,732 sq km

Region: Southeast

ARKANSAS
Little Rock

CALIFORNIA

Date of Statehood: 1850

Nickname: Golden State

Population: 36,132,147

Area: 163,696 sq mi; 423,970 sq km

Region: West

Sacramento
CALIFORNIA

COLORADO

Date of Statehood: 1876

Nickname: Centennial State

Population: 4,665,177

Area: 104,094 sq mi; 269,601 sq km

Region: West

Denver
COLORADO

CONNECTICUT

Date of Statehood: 1788

Nickname: Constitution State

Population: 3,510,297

Area: 5,543 sq mi; 14,357 sq km

Region: Northeast

Hartford
CONNECTICUT

DELAWARE

Date of Statehood: 1787

Nickname: First State

Population: 843,524

Area: 2,489 sq mi; 6,447 sq km

Region: Northeast

Dover
DELAWARE

FLORIDA

Date of Statehood: 1845

Nickname: Sunshine State

Population: 17,789,864

Area: 65,755 sq mi; 170,304 sq km

Region: Southeast

Tallahassee
FLORIDA

GEORGIA

Date of Statehood: 1788

Nickname: Peach State

Population: 9,072,576

Area: 59,425 sq mi; 153,909 sq km

Region: Southeast

Atlanta
GEORGIA

HAWAII

Date of Statehood: 1959

Nickname: The Aloha State

Population: 1,275,194

Area: 10,931 sq mi; 28,311 sq km

Region: West

Honolulu
HAWAII

IDAHO

Date of Statehood: 1890

Nickname: Gem State

Population: 1,429,096

Area: 83,570 sq mi; 216,446 sq km

Region: West

Boise
IDAHO

ILLINOIS

Date of Statehood: 1818

Nickname: The Prairie State

Population: 2,763,371

Area: 57,914 sq mi; 149,998 sq km

Region: Midwest

ILLINOIS
Springfield

INDIANA

Date of Statehood: 1816

Nickname: Hoosier State

Population: 6,271,973

Area: 36,418 sq mi; 94,321 sq km

Region: Midwest

INDIANA
Indianapolis

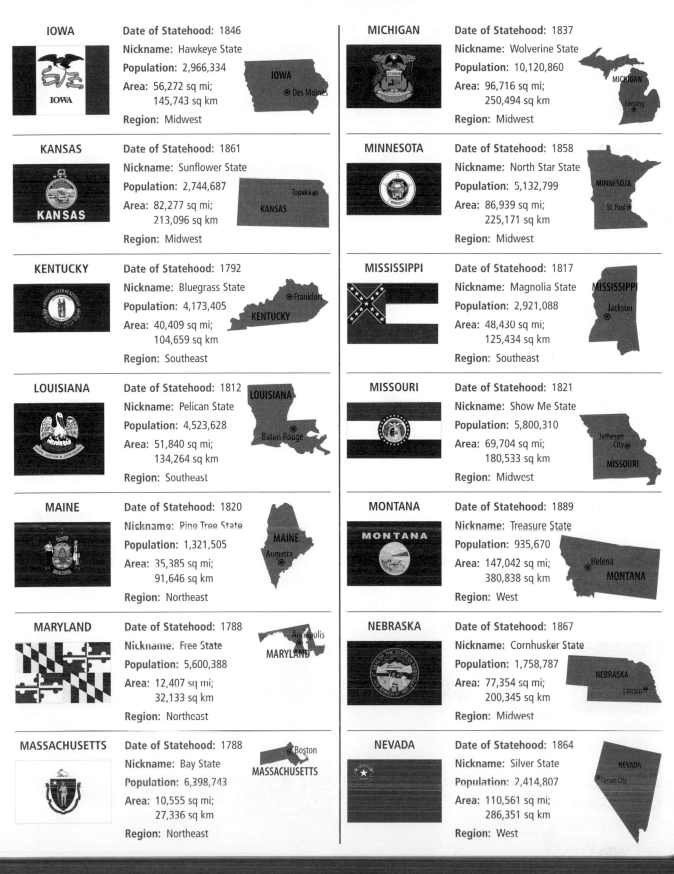

IOWA
Date of Statehood: 1846
Nickname: Hawkeye State
Population: 2,966,334
Area: 56,272 sq mi;
145,743 sq km
Region: Midwest

IOWA
⊛ Des Moines

KANSAS
Date of Statehood: 1861
Nickname: Sunflower State
Population: 2,744,687
Area: 82,277 sq mi;
213,096 sq km
Region: Midwest

Topeka ⊛
KANSAS

KENTUCKY
Date of Statehood: 1792
Nickname: Bluegrass State
Population: 4,173,405
Area: 40,409 sq mi;
104,659 sq km
Region: Southeast

⊛ Frankfort
KENTUCKY

LOUISIANA
Date of Statehood: 1812
Nickname: Pelican State
Population: 4,523,628
Area: 51,840 sq mi;
134,264 sq km
Region: Southeast

LOUISIANA
Baton Rouge ⊛

MAINE
Date of Statehood: 1820
Nickname: Pine Tree State
Population: 1,321,505
Area: 35,385 sq mi;
91,646 sq km
Region: Northeast

MAINE
Augusta ⊛

MARYLAND
Date of Statehood: 1788
Nickname: Free State
Population: 5,600,388
Area: 12,407 sq mi;
32,133 sq km
Region: Northeast

Annapolis ⊛
MARYLAND

MASSACHUSETTS
Date of Statehood: 1788
Nickname: Bay State
Population: 6,398,743
Area: 10,555 sq mi;
27,336 sq km
Region: Northeast

⊛ Boston
MASSACHUSETTS

MICHIGAN
Date of Statehood: 1837
Nickname: Wolverine State
Population: 10,120,860
Area: 96,716 sq mi;
250,494 sq km
Region: Midwest

MICHIGAN
Lansing ⊛

MINNESOTA
Date of Statehood: 1858
Nickname: North Star State
Population: 5,132,799
Area: 86,939 sq mi;
225,171 sq km
Region: Midwest

MINNESOTA
St. Paul ⊛

MISSISSIPPI
Date of Statehood: 1817
Nickname: Magnolia State
Population: 2,921,088
Area: 48,430 sq mi;
125,434 sq km
Region: Southeast

MISSISSIPPI
Jackson ⊛

MISSOURI
Date of Statehood: 1821
Nickname: Show Me State
Population: 5,800,310
Area: 69,704 sq mi;
180,533 sq km
Region: Midwest

Jefferson City ⊛
MISSOURI

MONTANA
Date of Statehood: 1889
Nickname: Treasure State
Population: 935,670
Area: 147,042 sq mi;
380,838 sq km
Region: West

Helena ⊛
MONTANA

NEBRASKA
Date of Statehood: 1867
Nickname: Cornhusker State
Population: 1,758,787
Area: 77,354 sq mi;
200,345 sq km
Region: Midwest

NEBRASKA
Lincoln ⊛

NEVADA
Date of Statehood: 1864
Nickname: Silver State
Population: 2,414,807
Area: 110,561 sq mi;
286,351 sq km
Region: West

NEVADA
⊛ Carson City

NEW HAMPSHIRE

Date of Statehood: 1788
Nickname: Granite State
Population: 1,309,940
Area: 9,350 sq mi;
24,216 sq km
Region: Northeast

NEW HAMPSHIRE
Concord

NEW JERSEY

Date of Statehood: 1787
Nickname: Garden State
Population: 8,717,925
Area: 8,721 sq mi;
22,588 sq km
Region: Northeast

Trenton
NEW JERSEY

NEW MEXICO

Date of Statehood: 1912
Nickname: Land of Enchantment
Population: 1,928,384
Area: 121,590 sq mi;
314,915 sq km
Region: Southwest

Santa Fe
NEW MEXICO

NEW YORK

Date of Statehood: 1788
Nickname: Empire State
Population: 19,254,630
Area: 54,556 sq mi;
141,299 sq km
Region: Northeast

Albany
NEW YORK

NORTH CAROLINA

Date of Statehood: 1789
Nickname: Tar Heel State
Population: 8,683,242
Area: 53,819 sq mi;
139,389 sq km
Region: Southeast

Raleigh
NORTH CAROLINA

NORTH DAKOTA

Date of Statehood: 1889
Nickname: Peace Garden State
Population: 636,677
Area: 70,700 sq mi;
183,112 sq km
Region: Midwest

NORTH DAKOTA
Bismarck

OHIO

Date of Statehood: 1803
Nickname: Buckeye State
Population: 11,464,042
Area: 44,825 sq mi;
116,096 sq km
Region: Midwest

OHIO
Columbus

OKLAHOMA

Date of Statehood: 1907
Nickname: Sooner State
Population: 3,547,884
Area: 69,898 sq mi;
181,036 sq km
Region: Southwest

OKLAHOMA
Oklahoma City

OREGON

Date of Statehood: 1859
Nickname: Beaver State
Population: 3,641,056
Area: 98,381 sq mi;
254,805 sq km
Region: West

Salem
OREGON

PENNSYLVANIA

Date of Statehood: 1787
Nickname: Keystone State
Population: 12,429,616
Area: 46,055 sq mi;
119,283 sq km
Region: Northeast

PENNSYLVANIA
Harrisburg

RHODE ISLAND

Date of Statehood: 1790
Nickname: Ocean State
Population: 1,076,189
Area: 1,545 sq mi;
4,002 sq km
Region: Northeast

RHODE ISLAND
Providence

SOUTH CAROLINA

Date of Statehood: 1788
Nickname: Palmetto State
Population: 4,255,083
Area: 32,020 sq mi;
82,932 sq km
Region: Southeast

Columbia
SOUTH CAROLINA

SOUTH DAKOTA

Date of Statehood: 1889
Nickname: Mount Rushmore State
Population: 775,933
Area: 77,117 sq mi;
199,731 sq km
Region: Midwest

Pierre
SOUTH DAKOTA

TENNESSEE

Date of Statehood: 1796
Nickname: Volunteer State
Population: 5,962,959
Area: 42,143 sq mi;
109,151 sq km
Region: Southeast

Nashville
TENNESEE

TEXAS
Date of Statehood: 1845
Nickname: Lone Star State
Population: 22,859,968
Area: 268,581 sq mi;
695,621 sq km
Region: Southwest

TEXAS
⊛ Austin

UTAH
Date of Statehood: 1896
Nickname: Beehive State
Population: 2,469,585
Area: 84,899 sq mi;
219,887 sq km
Region: West

Salt Lake City
UTAH

VERMONT
Date of Statehood: 1791
Nickname: Green Mountain State
Population: 623,050
Area: 9,614 sq mi;
24,901 sq km
Region: Northeast

VERMONT
⊛ Montpelier

VIRGINIA
Date of Statehood: 1788
Nickname: Old Dominion
Population: 7,567,465
Area: 42,774 sq mi;
110,785 sq km
Region: Southeast

Richmond ⊛
VIRGINIA

WASHINGTON
Date of Statehood: 1889
Nickname: Evergreen State
Population: 6,287,759
Area: 71,300 sq mi;
184,665 sq km
Region: West

⊛ Olympia
WASHINGTON

WEST VIRGINIA
Date of Statehood: 1863
Nickname: Mountain State
Population: 1,816,856
Area: 24,230 sq mi;
62,755 sq km
Region: Southeast

WEST VIRGINIA
⊛ Charleston

WISCONSIN
Date of Statehood: 1848
Nickname: Badger State
Population: 5,536,201
Area: 65,498 sq mi;
169,639 sq km
Region: Midwest

WISCONSIN
⊛ Madison

WYOMING
Date of Statehood: 1890
Nickname: Equality State
Population: 509,294
Area: 97,814 sq mi;
253,336 sq km
Region: West

WYOMING
Cheyenne ⊛

U.S. Commonwealth and Territories

AMERICAN SAMOA (U.S. TERRITORY)
Population: 57,881
Area: 77 sq mi;
199 sq km
Location: Pacific Ocean

GUAM (U.S. TERRITORY)
Population: 168,564
Area: 212 sq mi;
549 sq km
Location: Pacific Ocean

NORTHERN MARIANA ISLANDS (COMMONWEALTH)

Population: 80,362
Area: 184 sq mi;
477 sq km
Location: Pacific Ocean

PUERTO RICO (U.S. TERRITORY)
Population: 3,911,000
Area: 3,515 sq mi;
9,104 sq km
Location: Caribbean Sea

U.S. VIRGIN ISLANDS (U.S. TERRITORY)
Population: 108,708
Area: 136 sq mi;
352 sq km
Location: Caribbean Sea

Countries of the World

AFGHANISTAN

Capital: Kabul

Population: 29.9 million

Major languages: Dari, Pashto

Area: 251,772 sq mi; 652,086 sq km

LOCATION: Asia

ALBANIA

Capital: Tiranë

Population: 3.2 million

Major languages: Albanian

Area: 11,100 sq mi; 28,749 sq km

Location: Europe

ALGERIA

Capital: Algiers

Population: 32.8 million

Major Language: Arabic

Area: 919,591 sq mi; 2,381,730 sq km

Location: Africa

ANDORRA

Capital: Andorra la Vella

Population: 100,000

Major Language: Catalan

Area: 174 sq mi; 451 sq km

Location: Europe

ANGOLA

Capital: Luanda

Population: 15.4 million

Major Language: Portuguese

Area: 481,351 sq mi; 1,246,693 sq km

Location: Africa

ANTIGUA AND BARBUDA

Capital: St. John's

Population: 100,000

Major Language: English

Area: 170 sq mi; 440 sq km

Location: Caribbean Sea

ARGENTINA

Capital: Buenos Aires

Population: 38.6 million

Major Language: Spanish

Area: 1,073,514 sq mi; 2,780,388 sq km

Location: South America

ARMENIA

Capital: Yerevan

Population: 3.0 million

Major Language: Armenian

Area: 11,506 sq mi; 29,800 sq km

Location: Asia

AUSTRALIA

Capital: Canberra

Population: 20.4 million

Major Language: English

Area: 2,988,888 sq mi; 7,741,184 sq km

Location: Pacific Ocean

AUSTRIA

Capital: Vienna

Population: 8.2 million

Major Language: German

Area: 32,378 sq mi; 83,859 sq km

Location: Europe

AZERBAIJAN

Capital: Baku

Population: 8.4 million

Major Language: Azerbaijan

Area: 33,436 sq mi; 86,599 sq km

Location: Asia

BAHAMAS

Capital: Nassau

Population: 300,000

Major Language: English

Area: 5,359 sq mi; 13,880 sq km

Location: Caribbean Sea

BAHRAIN

Capital: Manama

Population: 700,000

Major Language: Arabic

Area: 266 sq mi; 689 sq km

Location: Asia

BANGLADESH

Capital: Dhaka

Population: 144.2 million

Major Language: Bengali

Area: 55,598 sq mi; 143,998 sq km

Location: Asia

BARBADOS

Capital: Bridgetown

Population: 300,000

Major Language: English

Area: 166 sq mi; 430 sq km

Location: Caribbean Sea

BELARUS

Capital: Minsk

Population: 9.8 million

Major Language: Belarusian

Area: 80,154 sq mi; 207,598 sq km

Location: Europe

BELGIUM

Capital: Brussels

Population: 10.5 million

Major Languages: Dutch, French, German

Area: 11,787 sq mi; 30,528 sq km

Location: Europe

BELIZE

Capital: Belmopan

Population: 300,000

Major Language: English

Area: 8,865 sq mi; 22,960 sq km

Location: North America

BENIN

Capital: Porto-Novo
Population: 8.4 million
Major Language: French
Area: 43,483 sq mi; 112,620 sq km
Location: Africa

BHUTAN

Capital: Thimphu
Population: 1.0 million
Major Language: Dzongkha
Area: 18,147 sq mi; 47,001 sq km
Location: Asia

BOLIVIA

Capitals: Sucre and La Paz
Population: 8.9 million
Major Languages: Spanish, Quechua, Aymara
Area: 424,162 sq mi; 1,098,574 sq km
Location: South America

BOSNIA AND HERZEGOVINA

Capital: Sarajevo
Population: 3.8 million
Major Language: Bosnian
Area: 19,741 sq mi; 51,129 sq km
Location: Europe

BOTSWANA

Capital: Gaborone
Population: 1.6 million
Major Languages: English, Setswana
Area: 224,606 sq mi; 581,727 sq km
Location: Africa

BRAZIL

Capital: Brasilia
Population: 184.2 million
Major Language: Portuguese
Area: 3,300,154 sq mi; 8,547,359 sq km
Location: South America

BRUNEI

Capital: Bandar Seri Begawan
Population: 400,000
Major Language: Malay
Area: 2,228 sq mi; 5,570 sq km
Location: Asia

BULGARIA

Capital: Sofia
Population: 7.7 million
Major Language: Bulgarian
Area: 42,822 sq mi; 110,908 sq km
Location: Europe

BURKINA FASO

Capital: Ouagadougou
Population: 13.9 million
Major Language: French
Area: 105,792 sq mi; 274,000 sq km
Location: Africa

BURUNDI

Capital: Bujumbura
Population: 7.8 million
Major Languages: Kirundi, French
Area: 10,745 sq mi; 27,829 sq km
Location: Africa

CAMBODIA

Capital: Phnom Penh
Population: 13.3 million
Major Language: Khmer
Area: 69,900 sq mi; 181,040 sq km
Location: Asia

CAMEROON

Capital: Yaoundé
Population: 16.4 million
Major Languages: English, French
Area: 183,568 sq mi; 475,439 sq km
Location: Africa

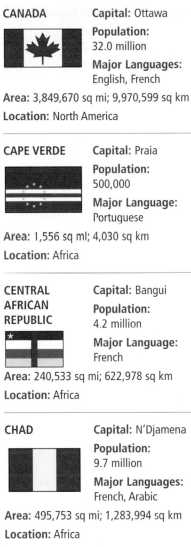

CANADA
Capital: Ottawa
Population: 32.0 million
Major Languages: English, French
Area: 3,849,670 sq mi; 9,970,599 sq km
Location: North America

CAPE VERDE
Capital: Praia
Population: 500,000
Major Language: Portuguese
Area: 1,556 sq mi; 4,030 sq km
Location: Africa

CENTRAL AFRICAN REPUBLIC
Capital: Bangui
Population: 4.2 million
Major Language: French
Area: 240,533 sq mi; 622,978 sq km
Location: Africa

CHAD
Capital: N'Djamena
Population: 9.7 million
Major Languages: French, Arabic
Area: 495,753 sq mi; 1,283,994 sq km
Location: Africa

CHILE
Capital: Santiago
Population: 16.1 million
Major Language: Spanish
Area: 292,135 sq mi; 756,626 sq km
Location: South America

CHINA
Capital: Beijing
Population: 1,303,700,000
Major Language: Mandarin Chinese
Area: 3,696,100 sq mi; 9,572,855 sq km
Location: Asia

COLOMBIA

Capital: Bogotá
Population: 46.0 million
Major Language: Spanish
Area: 439,734 sq mi; 1,138,906 sq km
Location: South America

COMOROS

Capital: Moroni
Population: 700,000
Major Languages: Arabic, French
Area: 861 sq mi; 2,230 sq km
Location: Indian Ocean

DEMOCRATIC REPUBLIC OF THE CONGO

Capital: Kinshasa
Population: 60.8 million
Major Language: French
Area: 905,351 sq mi; 2,344,848 sq km
Location: Africa

REPUBLIC OF THE CONGO

Capital: Brazzaville
Population: 4.0 million
Major Language: French
Area: 132,046 sq mi; 341,998 sq km
Location: Africa

COSTA RICA

Capital: San José
Population: 4.3 million
Major Language: Spanish
Area: 19,730 sq mi; 51,100 sq km
Location: North America

CÔTE D'IVOIRE
Capital: Yamoussoukro
Population: 18.2 million
Major Language: French
Area: 124,502 sq mi; 322,459 sq km
Location: Africa

CROATIA

Capital: Zagreb
Population: 4.4 million
Major Language: Croatian
Area: 21,830 sq mi; 56,539 sq km
Location: Europe

CUBA

Capital: Havana
Population: 11.3 million
Major Language: Spanish
Area: 42,803 sq mi; 110,859 sq km
Location: Caribbean Sea

CYPRUS

Capital: Nicosia
Population: 1.0 million
Major Language: Greek
Area: 3,571 sq mi; 9,249 kq km
Location: Mediterranean Sea

CZECH REPUBLIC

Capital: Prague
Population: 10.2 million
Major Language: Czech
Area: 30,448 sq mi; 78,860 sq km
Location: Europe

DENMARK

Capital: Copenhagen
Population: 5.4 million
Major Language: Danish
Area: 16,637 sq mi; 43,090 sq km
Location: Europe

DJIBOUTI

Capital: Djibouti
Population: 800,000
Major Languages: French, Arabic
Area: 8,958 sq mi; 23,201 sq km
Location: Africa

DOMINICA

Capital: Roseau
Population: 100,000
Major Language: English
Area: 290 sq mi; 751 sq km
Location: Caribbean Sea

DOMINICAN REPUBLIC

Capital: Santo Domingo
Population: 8.9 million
Major Language: Spanish
Area: 18,815 sq mi; 48,731 sq km
Location: Caribbean Sea

EAST TIMOR

Capital: Dili
Population: 900,000
Major Languages: Tetum, Portuguese
Area: 5,741 sq mi; 14,869 sq km
Location: Asia

ECUADOR

Capital: Quito
Population: 13.0 million
Major Language: Spanish
Area: 109,483 sq mi; 283,560 sq km
LOCATION: South America

EGYPT

Capital: Cairo
Population: 74 million
Major Language: Arabic
Area: 386,660 sq mi; 1,001,445 sq km
Location: Africa

EL SALVADOR

Capital: San Salvador
Population: 6.9 million
Major Language: Spanish
Area: 8,124 sq mi; 21,041 sq km
Location: North America

EQUATORIAL GUINEA

Capital: Malabo
Population: 500,000
Major Languages: Spanish, French
Area: 10,830 sq mi; 28,050 sq km
Location: Africa

ERITREA

Capital: Asmara
Population: 4.7 million
Major Language: Afar
Area: 45,405 sq mi; 117,598 sq km
Location: Africa

ESTONIA

Capital: Tallinn
Population: 1.3 million
Major Language: Estonian
Area: 17,413 sq mi; 45,099 sq km
Location: Europe

ETHIOPIA

Capital: Addis Ababa
Population: 77.4 million
Major Language: Amharic
Area: 426,371 sq mi; 1,104,296 sq km
Location: Africa

FIJI

Capital: Suva
Population: 800,000
Major Language: English
Area: 7,054 sq mi; 18,270 sq km
Location: Pacific Ocean

FINLAND

Capital: Helsinki
Population: 5.2 million
Major Languages: Finnish, Swedish
Area: 130,560 sq mi; 338,149 sq km
Location: Europe

FRANCE

Capital: Paris
Population: 60.7 million
Major Language: French
Area: 212,934 sq mi; 551,497 sq km
Location: Europe

GABON

Capital: Libreville
Population: 1.4 million
Major Language: French
Area: 103,347 sq mi; 267.667 sq km
Location: Africa

GAMBIA

Capital: Banjul
Population: 1.6 million
Major Language: English
Area: 4,363 sq mi; 11,300 sq km
Location: Africa

GEORGIA

Capital: Tbilisi
Population: 4.5 million
Major Language: Georgian
Area: 26,911 sq mi; 69,699 sq km
Location: Asia

GERMANY

Capital: Berlin
Population: 82.5 million
Major Language: German
Area: 137,830 sq mi; 356,978 sq km
Location: Europe

GHANA

Capital: Accra
Population: 22 million
Major Language: English
Area: 92,100 sq mi; 238,538 sq km
Location: Africa

GREECE
Capital: Athens
Population: 11.1 million
Major Language: Greek
Area: 50,950 sq mi; 131,960 sq km
Location: Europe

GRENADA
Capital: St. George's
Population: 100,000
Major Language: English
Area: 131 sq mi; 339 sq km
Location: Caribbean Sea

GUATEMALA
Capital: Guatemala City
Population: 12.7 million
Major Language: Spanish
Area: 42,042 sq mi; 108,888 sq km
Location: North America

GUINEA
Capital: Conakry
Population: 9.5 million
Major Language: French
Area: 94,927 sq mi; 245,860 sq km
Location: Africa

GUINEA-BISSAU
Capital: Bissau
Population: 1.6 million
Major Language: Portuguese
Area: 13,946 sq mi; 36,120 sq km
Location: Africa

GUYANA
Capital: Georgetown
Population: 800,000
Major Language: English
Area: 83,000 sq mi; 214,969 sq km
Location: South America

HAITI

Capital: Port-au-Prince
Population: 8.3 million
Major Languages: French, Creole
Area: 10,714 sq mi; 27,749 sq km
Location: Caribbean Sea

HONDURAS

Capital: Tegucigalpa
Population: 7.2 million
Major Language: Spanish
Area: 43,278 sq mi; 112,090 sq km
Location: North America

HUNGARY

Capital: Budapest
Population: 10.1 million
Major Language: Hungarian
Area: 35,919 sq mi; 93,030 sq km
Location: Europe

ICELAND

Capital: Reykjavik
Population: 300,000
Major Language: Icelandic
Area: 39,768 sq mi; 102,999 sq km
Location: Europe

INDIA

Capital: New Delhi
Population: 1,103,600,000
Major Languages: Hindi, English
Area: 1,269,340 sq mi; 3,287,575 sq km
Location: Asia

INDONESIA

Capital: Jakarta
Population: 221.9 million
Major Language: Bahasa Indonesia
Area: 735,355 sq mi; 1,904,561 sq km
Location: Asia

IRAN

Capital: Tehran
Population: 69.5 million
Major Language: Persian
Area: 630,575 sq mi; 1,633,182 sq km
Location: Asia

IRAQ

Capital: Baghdad
Population: 28.8 million
Major Language: Arabic
Area: 169,236 sq mi; 438,319 sq km
Location: Asia

IRELAND

Capital: Dublin
Population: 4.1 million
Major Languages: English, Irish
Area: 27,135 sq mi; 70,279 sq km
Location: Europe

ISRAEL

Capital: Jerusalem
Population: 7.1 million
Major Language: Hebrew
Area: 8,131 sq mi; 21,059 sq km
Location: Asia

ITALY

Capital: Rome
Population: 58.7 million
Major Language: Italian
Area: 116,320 sq mi; 301,267 sq km
Location: Europe

JAMAICA

Capital: Kingston
Population: 2.7 million
Major Language: English
Area: 4,243 sq mi; 10,989 sq km
Location: Caribbean Sea

JAPAN

Capital: Tokyo
Population: 127.7 million
Major Language: Japanese
Area: 145,869 sq mi; 377,799 sq km
Location: Asia

JORDAN

Capital: Amman
Population: 5.8 million
Major Language: Arabic
Area: 31,444 sq mi; 81,440 sq km
Location: Asia

KAZAKHSTAN

Capital: Astana
Population: 15.1 million
Major Languages: Kazakh, Russian
Area: 1,049,151 sq mi; 2,717,289 sq km
Location: Asia

KENYA

Capital: Nairobi
Population: 33.8 million
Major Languages: English, Kiswahili
Area: 224,081 sq mi; 580,367 sq km
Location: Africa

KIRIBATI

Capital: Tarawa (Bairiki)
Population: 100,000
Major Languages: I-Kiribati, English
Area: 282 sq mi; 730 sq km
Location: Pacific Ocean

KOREA, NORTH

Capital: Pyongyang
Population: 22.9 million
Major Language: Korean
Area: 46,541 sq mi; 120,541 sq km
Location: Asia

KOREA, SOUTH

Capital: Seoul
Population: 48.3 million
Major Language: Korean
Area: 38,324 sq mi; 99,259 sq km
Location: Asia

KUWAIT

Capital: Kuwait
Population: 2.6 million
Major Language: Arabic
Area: 6,880 sq mi; 17,819 sq km
Location: Asia

KYRGYZSTAN

Capital: Bishkek
Population: 5.2 million
Major Languages: Kyrgyz, Russian
Area: 76,641 sq mi; 198,499 sq km
Location: Asia

LAOS
Capital: Vientiane
Population: 5.9 million
Major Language: Lao
Area: 91,429 sq mi; 236,800 sq km
Location: Asia

LATVIA

Capital: Riga
Population: 2.3 million
Major Language: Latvian
Area: 24,942 sq mi; 64,599 sq km
Location: Europe

LEBANON

Capital: Beirut
Population: 3.8 million
Major Language: Arabic
Area: 4,015 sq mi; 10,399 sq km
Location: Asia

LESOTHO
Capital: Maseru
Population: 1.8 million
Major Languages: Sesotho, English
Area: 11,718 sq mi; 30,349 sq km
Location: Africa

LIBERIA
Capital: Monrovia
Population: 3.3 million
Major Language: English
Area: 43,000 sq mi; 111,369 sq km
Location: Africa

LIBYA
Capital: Tripoli
Population: 5.8 million
Major Language: Arabic
Area: 679,359 sq mi; 1,759,532 sq km
Location: Africa

LIECHTENSTEIN

Capital: Vaduz
Population: 40,000
Major Language: German
Area: 62 sq mi; 161 sq km
Location: Europe

LITHUANIA
Capital: Vilnius
Population: 3.4 million
Major Language: Lithuanian
Area: 25,174 sq mi; 65,200 sq km
Location: Europe

LUXEMBOURG

Capital: Luxembourg
Population: 500,000
Major Languages: Luxembourgish, German, French
Area: 999 sq mi; 2,587 sq km
Location: Europe

MACEDONIA
Capital: Skopje
Population: 2.0 million
Major Language: Macedonian
Area: 9,927 sq mi; 25,711 sq km
Location: Europe

MADAGASCAR
Capital: Antananarivo
Population: 17.3 million
Major Languages: French, Malagasy
Area: 226,656 sq mi; 587,036 sq km
Location: Indian Ocean

MALAWI
Capital: Lilongwe
Population: 12.3 million
Major Language: Chichewa
Area: 45,745 sq mi; 118,479 sq km
Location: Africa

MALAYSIA
Capital: Kuala Lumpur
Population: 26.1 million
Major Language: Bahasa Melayu
Area: 127,317 sq mi; 329,750 sq km
Location: Asia

MALDIVES
Capital: Male
Population: 300,000
Major Language: Maldivian Dhivehi
Area: 116 sq mi; 300 sq km
Location: Indian Ocean

MALI
Capital: Bamako
Population: 13.5 million
Major Language: French
Area: 478,838 sq mi; 1,240,185 sq km
Location: Africa

MALTA
Capital: Valletta
Population: 400,000
Major Languages: Maltese, English
Area: 124 sq mi; 321 sq km
Location: Mediterranean Sea

MARSHALL ISLANDS
Capital: Majuro
Population: 100,000
Major Languages: Marshallese, English
Area: 69 sq mi; 179 sq km
Location: Pacific Ocean

MAURITANIA
Capital: Nouakchott
Population: 3.1 million
Major Language: Arabic
Area: 395,954 sq mi; 1,025,516 sq km
Location: Africa

MAURITIUS
Capital: Port Louis
Population: 1.2 million
Major Languages: Creole, English
Area: 788 sq mi; 2,041 sq km
Location: Africa

MEXICO
Capital: Mexico City
Population: 107.0 million
Major Language: Spanish
Area: 756,082 sq mi; 1,958,243 sq km
Location: North America

FEDERATED STATES OF MICRONESIA
Capital: Palikir
Population: 100,000
Major Language: English
Area: 270 sq mi; 699 sq km
Location: Pacific Ocean

MOLDOVA
Capital: Chisinau
Population: 4.2 million
Major Language: Moldovan
Area: 13,012 sq mi; 33,701 sq km
Location: Europe

MONACO
Capital: Monaco
Population: 30,000
Major Language: French
Area: 1 sq mi; 2.6 sq km
Location: Europe

MONGOLIA
Capital: Ulaanbaatar
Population: 2.6 million
Major Language: Khalkha Mongol
Area: 604,826 sq mi; 1,566,492 sq km
Location: Asia

MONTENEGRO
Capital: Podgorica
Population: 650,000
Major Languages: Montenegrin, Serbian, Albanian
Area: 5,333 sq mi; 13,812 sq km
Location: Europe

MOROCCO
Capital: Rabat
Population: 30.7 million
Major Language: Arabic
Area: 172,413 sq mi; 446,548 sq km
Location: Africa

MOZAMBIQUE
Capital: Maputo
Population: 19.4 million
Major Language: Portuguese
Area: 309,494 sq mi; 801,586 sq km
Location: Africa

MYANMAR
Capital: Yangon (Rangoon)
Population: 50.5 million
Major Language: Burmese
Area: 261,228 sq mi; 676,577 sq km
Location: Asia

NAMIBIA
Capital: Windhoek
Population: 2.0 million
Major Language: English
Area: 318,259 sq mi; 824,287 sq km
Location: Africa

NAURU
Capital: Yaren
Population: 10,000
Major Language: Nauruan, English
Area: 9 sq mi; 23 sq km
Location: Pacific Ocean

NEPAL
Capital: Kathmandu
Population: 25.4 million
Major Language: Nepali
Area: 56,826 sq mi; 147,179 sq km
Location: Asia

NETHERLANDS
Capital: Amsterdam
Population: 16.4 million
Major Language: Dutch
Area: 13,082 sq mi; 33,883 sq km
Location: Europe

NEW ZEALAND
Capital: Wellington
Population: 4.1 million
Major Languages: English, Maori
Area: 104,452 sq mi; 270,529 sq km
Location: Pacific Ocean

NICARAGUA

Capital: Managua
Population: 5.8 million
Major Language: Spanish
Area: 50,193 sq mi; 129,999 sq km
Location: North America

NIGER

Capital: Niamey
Population: 14.0 million
Major Language: French
Area: 489,189 sq mi; 1,266,994 sq km
Location: Africa

NIGERIA

Capital: Abuja
Population: 131.5 million
Major Language: English
Area: 356,668 sq mi; 923,766 sq km
Location: Africa

NORWAY

Capital: Oslo
Population: 4.6 million
Major Language: Norwegian
Area: 125,050 sq mi; 323,878 sq km
Location: Europe

OMAN

Capital: Muscat
Population: 2.4 million
Major Language: Arabic
Area: 82,031 sq mi; 212,459 sq km
Location: Asia

PAKISTAN

Capital: Islamabad
Population: 162.4 million
Major Languages: Punjabi, Urdu, English
Area: 307,375 sq mi; 796,098 sq km
Location: Asia

PALAU

Capital: Koror
Population: 20,000
Major Languages: Palauan, English
Area: 178 sq mi; 461 sq km
Location: Pacific Ocean

PANAMA

Capital: Panama City
Population: 3.2 million
Major Language: Spanish
Area: 29,158 sq mi; 75,519 sq km
Location: North America

PAPAU NEW GUINEA

Capital: Port Moresby
Population: 5.9 million
Major Language: Melanesian Pidgin
Area: 178,703 sq mi; 462,839 sq km
Location: Pacific Ocean

PARAGUAY

Capital: Asunción
Population: 6.2 million
Major Languages: Spanish, Guarani
Area: 157,046 sq mi; 406,747 sq km
Location: South America

PERU

Capital: Lima
Population: 27.9 million
Major Languages: Spanish, Quechua
Area: 496,224 sq mi; 1,285,214 sq km
Location: South America

PHILIPPINES

Capital: Manila
Population: 84.8 million
Major Languages: Filipino, English
Area: 115,830 sq mi; 299,998 sq km
Location: Pacific Ocean

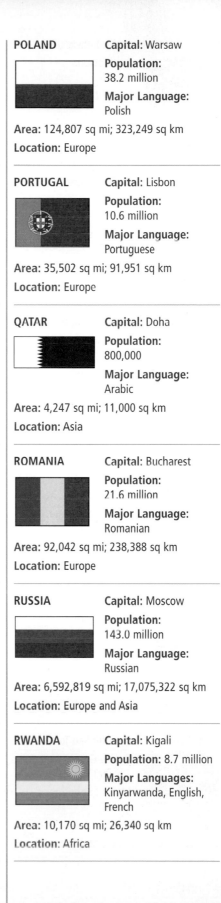

POLAND

Capital: Warsaw
Population: 38.2 million
Major Language: Polish
Area: 124,807 sq mi; 323,249 sq km
Location: Europe

PORTUGAL

Capital: Lisbon
Population: 10.6 million
Major Language: Portuguese
Area: 35,502 sq mi; 91,951 sq km
Location: Europe

QATAR

Capital: Doha
Population: 800,000
Major Language: Arabic
Area: 4,247 sq mi; 11,000 sq km
Location: Asia

ROMANIA

Capital: Bucharest
Population: 21.6 million
Major Language: Romanian
Area: 92,042 sq mi; 238,388 sq km
Location: Europe

RUSSIA

Capital: Moscow
Population: 143.0 million
Major Language: Russian
Area: 6,592,819 sq mi; 17,075,322 sq km
Location: Europe and Asia

RWANDA

Capital: Kigali
Population: 8.7 million
Major Languages: Kinyarwanda, English, French
Area: 10,170 sq mi; 26,340 sq km
Location: Africa

ST. KITTS-NEVIS

Capital: Basseterre
Population: 50,000
Major Language: English
Area: 139 sq mi; 360 sq km
Location: Caribbean Sea

ST. LUCIA

Capital: Castries
Population: 200,000
Major Language: English
Area: 239 sq mi; 619 sq km
Location: Caribbean Sea

ST. VINCENT AND THE GRENADINES

Capital: Kingstown
Population: 100,000
Major Language: English
Area: 151 sq mi; 391 sq km
Location: Caribbean Sea

SAMOA

Capital: Apia
Population: 200,000
Major Language: Samoan
Area: 1,097 sq mi; 2,841 sq km
Location: Pacific Ocean

SAN MARINO

Capital: San Marino
Population: 30,000
Major Language: Italian
Area: 23 sq mi; 60 sq km
Location: Europe

SÃO TOMÉ AND PRÍNCIPE

Capital: São Tomé
Population: 200,000
Major Language: Portuguese
Area: 371 sq mi; 961 sq km
Location: Gulf of Guinea, Africa

SAUDI ARABIA

Capital: Riyadh
Population: 24.6 million
Major Language: Arabic
Area: 829,996 sq mi; 2,149,680 sq km
Location: Asia

SENEGAL

Capital: Dakar
Population: 11.7 million
Major Language: French
Area: 75,954 sq mi; 196,720 sq km
Location: Africa

SERBIA AND MONTENEGRO

Capital: Belgrade
Population: 10.1 million
Major Language: Serbian
Area: 34,107 sq mi; 88,337 sq km
Location: Europe

SEYCHELLES

Capital: Victoria
Population: 100,000
Major Languages: Creole, English
Area: 174 sq mi; 451 sq km
Location: Indian Ocean

SIERRA LEONE

Capital: Freetown
Population: 5.5 million
Major Language: English
Area: 27,699 sq mi; 71,740 sq km
Location: Africa

SINGAPORE
Capital: Singapore
Population: 4.3 million
Major Language: Mandarin
Area: 239 sq mi; 619 sq km
Location: Asia

SLOVAKIA

Capital: Bratislava
Population: 5.4 million
Major Language: Slovak
Area: 18,923 sq mi; 49,010 sq km
Location: Europe

SLOVENIA

Capital: Ljubljana
Population: 2.0 million
Major Language: Slovenian
Area: 7,819 sq mi; 20,251 sq km
Location: Europe

SOLOMON ISLANDS

Capital: Honiara
Population: 500,000
Major Language: Melanesian Pidgin, English
Area: 11,158 sq mi; 28,889 sq km
Location: Pacific Ocean

SOMALIA

Capital: Mogadishu
Population: 8.6 million
Major Language: Somali
Area: 246,201 sq mi; 637,658 sq km
Location: Africa

SOUTH AFRICA
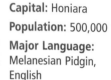
Capitals: Tshwane (Pretoria), Cape Town, Bloemfontein
Population: 46.9 million
Major Languages: Afrikaans, English, Zulu
Area: 471,444 sq mi; 1,221,034 sq km
Location: Africa

SPAIN
Capital: Madrid
Population: 43.5 million
Major Language: Spanish
Area: 193,363 sq mi; 500,808 sq km
Location: Europe

SRI LANKA

Capital: Colombo
Population: 19.7 million
Major Languages: Sinhala, Tamil, English
Area: 25,332 sq mi; 65,610 sq km
Location: Indian Ocean

SUDAN

Capital: Khartoum
Population: 40.2 million
Major Language: Arabic
Area: 967,494 sq mi; 2,505,798 sq km
Location: Africa

SURINAME

Capital: Paramaribo
Population: 438,000
Major Language: Dutch
Area: 62,344 sq mi; 161,470 sq km
Location: South America

SWAZILAND

Capital: Mbabane
Population: 1.138 million
Major Languages: English, siSwati
Area: 6,642 sq mi; 17,203 sq km
Location: Africa

SWEDEN

Capital: Stockholm
Population: 9.0 million
Major Language: Swedish
Area: 173,730 sq mi; 449,959 sq km
Location: Europe

SWITZERLAND
Capital: Bern
Population: 7.4 million
Major Languages: German, French, Italian
Area: 15,942 sq mi; 41,290 sq km
Location: Europe

SYRIA

Capital: Damascus
Population: 18.4 million
Major Language: Arabic
Area: 71,498 sq mi; 185,179 sq km
Location: Asia

TAIWAN

Capital: Taipei
Population: 22.7 million
Major Language: Mandarin Chinese
Area: 13,969 sq mi; 36,180 sq km
Location: Asia

TAJIKISTAN

Capital: Dushanbe
Population: 6.8 million
Major Language: Tajik
Area: 55,251 sq mi; 143,099 sq km
Location: Asia

TANZANIA

Capitals: Dar es Salaam, Dodoma
Population: 36.5 million
Major Languages: Kiswahili, English
Area: 364,900 sq mi; 945,087 sq km
Location: Africa

THAILAND

Capital: Bangkok
Population: 65.0 million
Major Language: Thai
Area: 198,116 sq mi; 513,118 sq km
Location: Asia

TOGO

Capital: Lomé
Population: 6.1 million
Major Language: French
Area: 21,927 sq mi; 56,791 sq km
Location: Africa

TONGA

Capital: Nuku'alofa
Population: 100,000
Major Language: Tongan, English
Area: 290 sq mi; 751 sq km
Location: Pacific Ocean

TRINIDAD AND TOBAGO

Capital: Port-of-Spain
Population: 1.3 million
Major Language: English
Area: 1,981 sq mi; 5,131 sq km
Location: Caribbean Sea

TUNISIA

Capital: Tunis
Population: 10.0 million
Major Languages: Arabic, French
Area: 63,170 sq mi; 163,610 sq km
Location: Africa

TURKEY

Capital: Ankara
Population: 72.9 million
Major Language: Turkish
Area: 299,158 sq mi; 774,816 sq km
Location: Asia and Europe

TURKMENISTAN

Capital: Ashkhabad
Population: 5.2 million
Major Language: Turkmen
Area: 188,456 sq mi; 488,099 sq km
Location: Asia

TUVALU

Capital: Funafuti
Population: 10,000
Major Language: Tuvaluan
Area: 10 sq mi; 26 sq km
Location: Pacific Ocean

UGANDA

Capital: Kampala
Population: 26.9 million
Major Language: English
Area: 93,066 sq mi; 241,040 sq km
Location: Africa

UKRAINE

Capital: Kyiv (Kiev)
Population: 47.1 million
Major Language: Ukrainian
Area: 233,089 sq mi; 603,698 sq km
Location: Europe

UNITED ARAB EMIRATES

Capital: Abu Dhabi
Population: 4.6 million
Major Language: Arabic
Area: 32,278 sq mi; 83,600 sq km
Location: Asia

UNITED KINGDOM

Capital: London
Population: 60.1 million
Major Language: English
Area: 94,548 sq mi; 244,878 sq km
Location: Europe

UNITED STATES

Capital: Washington, D.C.
Population: 296.5 million
Major Language: English
Area: 3,717,796 sq mi; 9,629,047 sq km
Location: North America

URUGUAY
Capital: Montevideo
Population: 3.4 million
Major Language: Spanish
Area: 68,498 sq mi; 177,409 sq km
Location: South America

UZBEKISTAN

Capital: Tashkent
Population: 26.4 million
Major Language: Uzbek
Area: 172,741 sq mi; 447,397 sq km
Location: Asia

VANUATU

Capital: Port-Vila
Population: 200,000
Major Languages: Local languages, Bislama
Area: 4,707 sq mi; 12,191 sq km
Location: Pacific Ocean

VATICAN CITY

Capital: Vatican City
Population: 1,000
Major Languages: Italian, Latin
Area: 1 sq mi; 2.6 sq km.
Location: Europe

VENEZUELA

Capital: Caracas
Population: 26.7 million
Major Language: Spanish
Area: 352,143 sq mi; 912,046 sq km
Location: South America

VIETNAM

Capital: Hanoi
Population: 83.3 million
Major Language: Vietnamese
Area: 128,066 sq mi; 331,689 sq km
Location: Asia

YEMEN

Capital: Sanaa
Population: 20.7 million
Major Language: Arabic
Area: 203,849 sq mi; 527,966 sq km
Location: Asia

ZAMBIA

Capital: Lusaka
Population: 11.2 million
Major Language: English
Area: 290,583 sq mi; 752,606 sq km
Location: Africa

ZIMBABWE
Capital: Harare
Population: 13.0 million
Major Language: English
Area: 150,873 sq mi; 390,759 sq km
Location: Africa

Index

Eureka, CA 22
Evansville, IN 22
Fairbanks, AK 8, 22
Fargo, ND 22
Fez 12
Fort Smith, AR 22
Fort Worth, TX 22
Frankfort, KY 22
Freetown 12
Fresno, CA 22
Funafuti 20
Gaborone 12
Gary, IN 22
Georgetown 10
Glasgow 14
Göteborg 14
Grand Forks, ND 22
Grand Rapids, MI 22
Great Falls, MT 22
Green Bay, WI 22
Guadalajara 8
Guangzhou 16
Guayaquil 10
Hagatna 20
Hamburg 14
Hanoi 16
Harare 12
Harbin 16
Harrisburg, PA 22
Hartford, CT 22
Helena, MT 22
Helsinki 14
Hilo, HI 22
Ho Chi Minh City 16
Hobart 20
Hong Kong 16
Honiara 20
Honolulu, HI 22, 28, 29
Houston, TX 8, 22, 28
Hue 16
Hyderabad 16
Indianapolis, IN 22, 28
Iqaluit 8
Iquitos 10
Irkutsk 16
Isfahan 16, 18
Islamabad 16
Istanbul 16, 28
Jabalpur 16
Jackson, MS 22
Jacksonville, FL 22, 28, 29
Jakarta 16, 28
Jefferson City, MO 22
Jerusalem 16, 18
Jinan 16
Johannesburg 12
Juneau, AK 8, 22
Kabul 16
Kampala 12
Kananga 12
Kandahar 16
Kano 12
Kansas City, KS 22
Kansas City, MO 22, 28
Karachi 16, 28
Kathmandu 16

Kazan 14
Khabarovsk 16
Kharkiv 14
Khartoum 12
Kiev 14
Kigali 12
Kinshasa 12
Kirkuk 18
Kisangani 12
Knoxville, TN 22
Kolkata (Calcutta) 16, 28
Krasnoyarsk 16
Kuala Lumpur 16
Kuwait 16, 18
Kyoto 16
La Paz 10
Laayoune 12
Lagos 12, 28
Lansing, MI 22
Laredo, TX 22
Las Vegas, NV 22, 28
Lhasa 16
Libreville 12
Lilongwe 12
Lima 10, 28
Lincoln, NE 22
Lisbon 14
Little Rock, AR 22
Liverpool 14
Ljubljana 14
_odz 14
Lome 12
London 14, 28
Long Beach, CA 22
Los Angeles, CA 8, 22, 28, 29
Louisville, KY 22
Luanda 12
Lusaka 12
Luxembourg 14
Macau 16
Madison, WI 22
Madrid 14
Magadan 16
Majuro 20
Malabo 12
Male 16
Manado 16
Manama 16, 18
Manaus 10
Mandalay 16
Manila 16, 28
Maputo 12
Maracaibo 10
Marquette, MI 22
Marrakech 12
Marseille 14
Maseru 12
Mashhad 18
Mawlamyine 16
Mbabane 12
Mecca 16, 18
Medellín 10
Medina 16, 18
Melbourne 20
Melekeok 20
Memphis, TN 22, 28

México City 8, 28
Miami, FL 8, 22, 28
Milan 14
Milwaukee, WI 22, 28
Minneapolis, MN 8, 22, 28
Minsk 14
Mobile, AL 22
Mogadishu 12
Mombasa 12
Monaco 14
Monrovia 12
Monterrey 8
Montevideo 10
Montgomery, AL 22
Montpelier, VT 22
Montréal 8
Moroni 12
Moscow 14, 16, 28
Mumbai (Bombay) 16, 28
Munich 14
Muscat 16, 18
N'Djamena 12
Nagasaki 16
Nairobi 12
Nanjing 16
Nantes 14
Naples 14
Nashville, TN 22
Naypydaw 16
New Delhi 16
New Orleans, LA 8, 22, 26, 28, 29
New York, NY 8, 22, 28, 29
Newark, NJ 22
Niamey 12
Nicosia 16, 18
Nizhniy Novgorod 14
Nome, AK 22, 29
Norfolk, VA 22
Nouakchott 12
Noumea 20
Nuku'alofa 20
Nuuk 8
Oakland, CA 22
Odessa 14
Ogden, UT 22
Oklahoma City, OK 22, 28
Olympia, WA 22
Omaha, NE 22, 28
Oran 12
Orlando, FL 22
Osaka 28
Oslo 14
Ottawa 8
Ouagadougou 12
Pago Pago 20
Palembang 16
Palikir 20
Papeete 20
Paramaribo 10
Paris 14, 28
Palma 16
Perth 20
Philadelphia, PA 8, 22, 28
Phnom Penh 16
Phoenix, AZ 8, 22, 28, 29
Pierre, SD 22

Pittsburgh, PA 22
Pocatello, ID 22
Podgorica 14
Port Elizabeth 12
Port Moresby 20
Port Sudan 12
Portland, ME 22
Portland, OR 8, 22, 28
Porto Alegre 10
Porto-Novo 12
Port-Vila 20
Prague 14
Pretoria 12
Providence, RI 22
Provo, UT 22
Pueblo, CO 22
Punta Arenas 10
Pyonqyang 16
Qaraghandy 16
Québec 8
Quezon City 16
Quito 10
Rabat 12
Raleigh, NC 22, 28
Recife 10
Redding, CA 22
Reno, NV 22
Reykjavik 14
Richmond, VA 22
Riga 14
Rio de Janeiro 10, 28
Riyadh 16, 18
Rome 14
Rosario 10
Rostov 14
Sacramento, CA 22
Salem, OR 22
Salt Lake City, UT 8, 22, 28
Salvador (Bahía) 10
Samara 14
San Antonio, TX 22, 28
San Diego, CA 22, 28
San Francisco, CA 8, 22, 26, 28, 29
San Jose, CA 22
Sanaa 16, 18
Santa Fe, NM 22
Santiago 10
São Paulo 10, 28
Sao Tome 12
Sapporo 16
Sarajevo 14
Saratov 14
Savannah, GA 22
Seattle, WA 8, 22, 28, 29
Semey 16
Seoul 16, 28
Shanghai 16, 28
Shreveport, LA 22
Singapore 16
Sioux Falls, SD 22
Skopje 14
Sofia 14
Spokane, WA 22
Springfield, IL 22
St. Louis, MO 8, 22, 28
St. Paul, MN 22

Bodies of Water